The Highest Apple

Sappho and The Lesbian Poetic Tradition

The Highest Apple

Sappho and The Lesbian Poetic Tradition

Judy Grahn

Spinsters, Ink
San Francisco

First Edition
10 - 9 - 8 - 7 - 6 - 5 - 4 - 3 - 2 - 1

Spinsters, Ink
803 De Haro Street
San Francisco, CA 94107

Cover and Interior Art: Karen Sjöholm
Cover Design: Linda Szyniszewski, Elephant Graphics
Author Photo: Irene Young
Design and Production: Sherry Thomas, Deborah DeBont, Sukey Wilder, and Kathy Jaramillo
Typesetting: Jean Swallow and ComText Typography, Inc.
Printed in the U.S.A.

The publication of this book is made possible by the generous support and assistance of Angels Ink, without whom it would not have been possible.

Publication was also made possible, in part, with public funds from the California Arts Council, which we gratefully acknowledge.

ISBN: 0 - 933216-12-2
Library of Congress Catalog Card Number:84-51941

The author gratefully acknowledges permission from the following sources to reprint material under their control:

Paula Gunn Allen for permission to quote from the following: "The Garden," "He Na Tye Woman," from *Shadow Country*, UCLA-Native American Series, 1982, with grateful acknowledgement to the Board of Regents, University of California, and the Native American Studies Center, UCLA. © Board of Regents, University of California, 1982. Lines from "The Trick Is Consciousness," from *Coyote's Daylight Trip*, La Confluencia, 1978 © Paula Gunn Allen. "Taku Skanskan," "Transitions," and lines from "Some Like Indians Endure," © Paula Gunn Allen. Exerpts from *The Woman Who Owned The Shadows* © 1983 Spinsters, Ink.

City Lights Books for exerpts from *Notes on Thought and Vision* by H.D., copyright, © by the Estate of Hilda Doolittle.

Copper Canyon Press for exerpts from *Pastoral Jazz* by Olga Broumas © 1983 Olga Broumas; Copper Canyon Press, P.O. Box 271, Port Townsend, Wa. 98368.

The Crossing Press for exerpts from *The Work of a Common Woman*, © 1978 Judy Grahn, including exerpts from the Introduction by Adrienne Rich. And exerpts from *Movement in Black*, © 1984 by Pat Parker. Both are from the Crossing Press Feminist Series, Trumansburg, NY, 14886.

Elsa Gidlow for an exerpt from "For the Goddess Too Well Known," first published in *On a Grey Thread* Elsa Gidlow's collection of lesbian poetry brought out by Will Ransom in 1923. Reprinted in *Sapphic Songs Seventeen to Seventy* a Gidlow collection from Diana Press in 1976, and *Sapphic Songs Eighteen to Eighty*, a larger collection of lesbian poetry © 1982 by Druid Heights Press.

Harvard University Press for exerpts from *Greek Lyric I*, translated by D.A. Campbell, reprinted by permission of the publishers and The Loeb Classical Library, Cambridge, Ma.: Harvard University Press, Copyright © 1982 by the President and Fellows of Harvard College. And for the following poems by Emily Dickinson: #1037, 239, 513, 1719, 636, and 1260, reprinted by permission of the publishers and the Trustees of Amherst College from *The Poems of Emily Dickinson*, edited by Thomas H. Johnson, Cambridge, Ma.: The Belknap Press of Harvard University Press, Copyright 1951, © 1955, 1979, 1983 by the President and Fellows of Harvard College.

To All Lovers

Acknowledgements

My thanks to Mary Carruthers for her crisp mind and definition of "Lesbian Poetry"; to Paula Gunn Allen as always for hours of exhilarating conversation, definitions of metaphysics and Hermeticism, for giving me access to her library of spiritual traditions and for teaching a course in comparative spiritualities; to Judith McDaniel for sending her precious copy of *Pictures of the Floating World*; to Adrienne Rich for a ms. copy of *Sources* and for wonderful praises as I went along; to Olga Broumas for generously sending ms. material; to Pat Parker for being a poet-comrade-in-arms in those early days when the going was really rough; to Sherry Thomas for loving belief in the ideas behind the work and for firm editorial guidance; to Karen Sjoholm for her friendship and magnificent cover art.

Thanks also to Betty Meadors for responding to the ideas of this book with a woman-based Jungian perspective. For supporting me (literally as well as psychologically) I am grateful to Beverly Tannenhaus and Katharyn Aal of the Women Writers Workshop and to Rita Speicher and Rachel DeVries of the (former) Women's Writers Center, both located in New York state.

I especially want to express appreciation to Duncan McNoughton, Diane DiPrima, Robert Duncan, David Meltzer, Louis Patler and Michael Harrington of the New College Poetics program for their support of this project — Duncan for hiring me to deliver three lectures on Sappho to his class; Diane for saying, when I said, "Oh I can't do that," "Oh of course you can." I just want to thank Diane for so often being there, ahead of me, and making a way for me.

Table of Contents

Introduction

I could never have written this little book without first writing another, much longer one, of which this was originally to have been a chapter — a chapter on Sappho and the importance of poetry to Lesbians. The long book took ten years of research and effort, and is called *Another Mother Tongue: Gay Words, Gay Worlds* (Boston: Beacon Press, 1984). By and large it is a Gay and Lesbian cultural history, a complex exploration of stories, myths and anthropological extrapolations concerning the possible meaning throughout history of certain words, phrases and odd character traits commonly associated with Gayness. These include purple as the "Gay color," little finger rings, and names such as dyke, faggot, round, fairy, buggery, butch and the like.

Another Mother Tongue proposes that Gay people have a culture, that it cuts across class, race, gender and even national and tribal categories. It proposes farther that Gay people have functions in society that involve, and in fact require, Gay attributes. In short, it says that Gay culture is central to Gay people and that Gay people are central to their societies, even when they occupy a despised or underground position. I have used that idea in *The Highest Apple* also, with an additional proposition that women, too, have a culture, a heritage and a central position with regard to their societies. I have gone even further; I have supposed that even poets have important positions in society, whether acknowledged or not; and that Sappho is a prime example of such a poet and of such a central position.

Sappho gave us several traditions, among them a tradition of poets of Love, hardly the least of her contributions. Though I am, in *The Highest Apple*, treating a very special tradition that she also gave us, a Sapphic tradition of woman-bonding, I want to give all my thanks to a Poetics department of love, the New College of California Poetics Program who made the essays possible, and who in every way carry on the tradition of poetry as a province of lovers — all lovers.

Lesbian culture may be seen as "marginal" by heterosexual culture and heterosexual definition, but surely Lesbian culture is central to Lesbians. Moreover, the work that comes from Lesbian culture, the special perspective, can be central to society as a whole. Especially if the women doing the work decide to give it that central direction. Both H.D.'s and Gertude Stein's bodies of work are as central to the literature — and consequently the philosophical understandings — of the twentieth century as Emily Dickinson (and Walt Whitman) were for the nineteenth. Their work is not marginal, their lives were not marginal to their society, though perhaps they lived an extreme synthesis of the lives of most of their compatriots.

"Marginal" is a word that implies, like the story of Columbus, that there is one world, and it is flat. At the edge is the "margin," occupied by those dangerous, powerless and (poor) oppressed groups who have so vehemently defined themselves in the American mind in this century: Black, Gay, Lesbian, Jewish, Indian, "Third World," the elderly, etc.

Fortunately, at the heart of these groups one finds an entirely different schema, a map virtually unrelated to the one held by the flat world folks. I first saw this new way of looking very clearly when I was a young woman living with my first lover, Von, in the city of Washington, D.C. Von taught physical education in the schools, and was one of those teachers assigned to a number of schools, eight in all. She saw quite a bit of the city, which in 1963 and 1964 was rapidly altering its racial composition. Hopeful Blacks pouring in from the South displaced much of Washington's white population, who fled in the face of their own racial fears and spectres. Housing speculators fed their panic and the rising hopes of the Blacks by doing "block busting," deliberately terrorizing the white homeowners with visions of losing everything to low-class ghetto dwellers, then re-selling the cheaply bought houses at inflated prices to incoming Black people. It was an ugly and often repeated American scene.

Von and I, like so many of our generation, were particularly sensitive and drawn to the situation of Black people, indeed of all the people defined as displaced, oppressed, "marginal". We identified with them, because we came from poor and immigrant backgrounds in our own families, and because we ourselves, as Lesbians and as single women, were defined and treated as marginal, displaced and oppressed.

Yet in the midst of this scenario, we spotted an entirely different one. We first heard the news on the radio; Washington's Black radio programming featured Elijah Muhammad, a fiery speaker of the Black Nation of Islam. "Black Nation" — we had never heard of such a thing. We were frightened at first, and curious. Then our attention riveted to a more worldly version of Black separatism in the person of Malcom X. He was electrifying, and we followed the tumultuous history of the Black Muslims not only for what Black people were learning but also for what we were learning from him, about the essential importance of autonomy, self-determination, and community. I could tell that separatism and the centrality of a group of people to themselves were powerful social tools. The assassination of Malcolm X was the first of that series of killings that pierced the Sixties with arrows of irrevocable determination and commitment. I remember experiencing his death as an understanding of the price of radical leadership, and that what we were — and are — involved in is a low-level ongoing war.

When five years later, in 1969, it was time for me to help form an organization that would further the development of Gay people, I joined with seven or eight other young women, several of whom had also experienced in one way or another the teachings of Malcolm X, and who also, like me, had been strongly influenced by the Lesbian underground network of bars, cliques and a magazine, *The Ladder*. Several of our number were Jewish radical Lesbians, including my lover at the time, Wendy Cadden. Some were from the European folk "marginal culture" known variously as lower class, working class, white trash, or even middle class in sociological jargon. Some were Black, including poet Pat Parker and an outspoken woman who changed her Anglo-Saxon name to Ama. The organizations we proceeded to define and develop were Lesbian separatist, with a feminist and radical underbase. From the meetings grew all-women's households, institutions in and of themselves, that gave rise to others, to newspapers, to the first all-women's bookstore (A Woman's Place in Oakland, CA), to the first all-women's press (The Women's Press Collective). Meetings of all kinds took place in the house, such as the first meeting of what became the Lesbian Mother's Union, called by Black Lesbian organizer Pat Norman, and dozens of other meetings ranging from prison organizing, to working for welfare rights, to anti-rape campaigns, to the editing of books and the promotion of artwork and literature.

Without our knowledge of the use of separatism we might still have been straining to get a word in edgewise at the large meetings of Gay men with tangential, yet different, concerns, needs and issues. Once we had our own concerns going we found that plenty of people wanted to listen to us. We had a voice.

We had a voice of our own, and when it spoke the first words were through the poets. Masses of women came to those early readings and even more masses came later when it became "the thing to do." Fifteen years later, and long after the women musicians and songwriters, the dramatists, film makers and comedians, political organizers and office holders have risen by the hundreds and thousands to fill in all the details of what we were barely outlining, "the movement" still keeps one ear to the ground to hear what else its poets may be telling. In every sense, we have been mediums. Involved in as much of our community as we could spare from our meditative work and the ever present necessity of earning a living and in some cases, raising children, we poets are sometimes exactly expressive of the communities we belong to, sometimes a little behind time, and many times ahead of time with private visions given from sources we ourselves are unable to explain.

The nine poets I have chosen to link in a tradition with Sappho have been picked carefully. Emily Dickinson, Amy Lowell, H.D. and Gertrude Stein are historic foremothers of today's Lesbian poets. The five contemporary women: Adrienne Rich, Audre Lorde, Olga Broumas, Paula Gunn Allen and myself were chosen after I was very positively influenced by an article in *The Hudson Review* by Professor Mary J. Carruthers of the University of Illinois at Chicago. Carruthers titled her essay, "The ReVision of the Muse: Adrienne Rich, Audre Lorde, Judy Grahn and Olga Broumas." She selected these particular people because, "These four poets have voices that are bold, even arrogant, in their common, urgent desire to seize the language and forge with it an instrument for articulating women. Not all women writing today write this kind of poetry, not all poets who are Lesbians are Lesbian poets, nor are all Lesbian poets always Lesbian." She goes on to state that the "naming and defining" of the word Lesbian is a central preoccupation of our work.[1]

We are using the word and the nature of Lesbian, of our special position as Lesbians, as a lens through which to examine the rest of our society. "The word *Lesbian* presents in paradigm the large issues of value in language, of women's psyche and of social transformation, of alienation and apocalypse, which these poets address."[2]

Even our position as outcast, a position well-articulated in our work, helps to give us the special eyes through which we see. Carruthers says "*Lesbian* is also the essential outsider, woman alone and integral, who is oppressed and despised by traditional society, yet thereby free to use her position to re-form and re-member. She is a figure both of the satirist and the seer, a woman of integrity and power who is by nature and choice at odds with the world. *Lesbian* is also erotic connection, the primary energy of the senses which is both physical and intellectual, connecting women, a woman with herself, and women through time. Finally, *Lesbian* signifies a change of relationships, radical internal transformation; it is a myth of psychic rebirth, social redemption, and apocalypse."[3] We seek, she says, nothing less than the total transformation of our society.

From these interesting definitions, I drew some criteria of my own with which to formulate the ideas I have set forth in *The Highest Apple*. The contemporary poets whose work I have chosen to discuss include all four of the ones included in Mary Carruther's analysis, plus Paula Gunn Allen, whose American Indian voice completes the picture of Lesbian presence on this American continent.

All of our work connects political, personal, sexual, historic and mythic themes. We are representative of scores of Lesbian poets specializing in various aspects of what we are all doing together. Lesbian poetry, as you will see, is witty, detailed, personal, sexy, mythic, biting, eloquent, aesthetic, and profound, as our lady Sappho was all these qualities also.

These essays make no attempt to provide a comprehensive overview of all the Lesbian poetry currently available in America. There are dozens of contemporary poets writing on Lesbian living, and Lesbians writing on contemporary living. Nor is this particular analysis attempting to specify "major" poets, nor in any way suggest that we current writers are to be compared with Sappho for her vitality. She is twenty-six centuries ahead of all of us, and is like a god to me. I am simply doing a comparison of ideas and themes as a way of beginning the outline for a Lesbian tradition of poetry. I selected the included voices on the basis of the fullness of their bodies of work, and of their development of certain ideas I wanted to pursue and compare. The primary story I am telling is of the re-emergence of the public Lesbian voice.

There is a tremendous need for some ambitious souls to undertake comprehensive and historical overviews of Lesbian content in women's poetry. There is a need for careful analysis and treatment of the work of such openly Lesbian poets as: Elsa Gidlow, who has published overtly Lesbian love poems since the 1920's, Pat Parker, Marilyn Hacker, Susan Griffin, Minnie Bruce Pratt, Cherríe Moraga, Joy Harjo, Chocolate Waters, Cheryl Clarke, Irena Klepfisz, Jan Clausen, Donna Allegra, and dozens of others.

Poetry is important to women, and it is especially important to Lesbians. More than one Lesbian has been kept from floundering on the rocks of alienation from her own culture, her own center, by having access, at least, to Lesbian poetry. We owe a great deal to poetry; two of our most important names, for instance: Lesbian and Sapphic. When has a larger group of humans, more pervasive behavior, and much more than this, the tradition of women's secret powers that such names imply, ever been named for a single poet? Through the centuries our poetry has held that position in the branches of its lines, in fragments, and in the code of imagery. It is time, now, to begin to reveal that tradition.

Notes:

1 Mary J. Carruthers, "The Re-Vision of the Muse: Adrienne Rich, Audre Lorde, Judy Grahn and Olga Broumas," *The Hudson Review*, Vol.XXXVI, Number 2, Summer 1983, p. 293.

2 Ibid., p. 294.

3 Ibid., pp. 294-95.

Part I

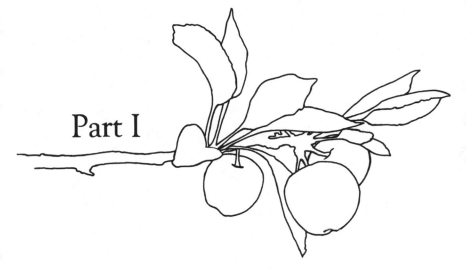

Heart Shaped Journey
To a Similar Place

A Heart Shaped Journey
To A Similar Place

And Sappho wrote this:

> *As the sweet-apple reddens on the bough-top, on the top of
> the topmost bough; the apple gatherers have forgotten it —
> no, they have not forgotten it entirely, but they could not
> reach it.*[1]

I want to tell you a story, a story that particularly underlies
much of the writing of the Lesbians of our era, as well as that of
those feminists who accept the evidence of ancient (as well as
modern) gynarchic societies. This is a story that says once upon a
time, the world was very different from ours in quite specific and
woman-related ways; in the world before and leading up to the
poet Sappho there was a very considerable time, millenia, during
which people were tribal and spiritual and their culture was based
primarily in womanly powers.

Elizabeth Gould Davis gave us this information in *The First
Sex* and Jane Ellen Harrison gave some confirmation of it in her
ponderous studies of Greek mythic history, as has Marija Gim-
butas with her archeology of ancient European gods, Evelyn Reed
with her Marxian view, and Mary Daly with her philosophical

unravellings of women's place in the universe. From Zora Neal Hurston and Margaret Murray we have gotten information of the Black and white folk customs, many of which stem from pagan religions that went underground not so long ago as we might think. Robert Graves and some of the Jungian writers have long sought to give The Great Goddess her rightful position in the Western mind. Charlene Spretnak, Starhawk, Z. Budapest, Luisah Teish and other women involved in what is generally called the "women's spirituality movement," along with modern Indian women such as Paula Gunn Allen and Joy Harjo and others writing about Indian women's traditions such as Lynn Andrews and Anne Cameron have added to our understanding. All are surfacing with thousands of particles of fact and impression, picture and intuition, tradition and story, to give us our understanding of the world as a long, long story, of which the four or five thousand year rise and spread of the patriarchal form is only one aspect, one era that developed within a complex matrix of other possible ways of being.

Our teachers have told that in those times in the ancient Mediterranean cultures that gave rise to Sappho, there were very great poets. Many of them, perhaps most of them, were women. We have been told that the goddess of India, Sarasvati, is the goddess of language and is a poet; she rides on a peacock because, just as a peacock's tail contains many eyes, so she, as a poet, needs many eyes to see all around herself deciphering what is true, or truly there for her perceiving. We know that the West African goddess Afrikete was goddess of language and poetry, as well as being a transvestite and a warrior, and that she preceeded the trickster god Eshu, who took over many of her former functions.[2] We know it is said of Arabia that before the rise of patriarchal systems, it was a woman-centered culture, and that the seven most wondrous poets of the ancient world were women, Arab women, and every word of their work was destroyed when the newly forming patriarchal elements found it too competitive with their own world-view.

The island of Lesbos has a long female-centered history, one more specifically remembered than some others, at least among Western peoples. Sappho's own home city of Mitylene was founded by Amazons who came from North Africa. After fighting their way across Arabia and Syria and establishing a shrine to Artemis at the city of Ephesos, they came across to the island of Lesbos where their leader, Myrina, established a special seaport city in honor of her sister Mitylene. Some six hundred years later, Sappho was born there. Described as being of small stature with a dark complexion, the earliest coin representation shows a sharp-nosed woman who resembles the frizzy-haired women of Crete as they portrayed themselves on the wall friezes. Sappho had a daughter, Cleis, who she praised in her poetry, and called "golden."

It is with these understandings in mind that I comprehend Sappho, not as the "first woman poet," but as the last of that great era, and the only one to have some fragments survive. It is with this millenia-long story in mind that I understand that both Homer and Sappho were drawing from, and writing out of, a vast, rich ancient and woman-developed tradition which they shared in common. A common pool of stories, phrases, metaphors, and philosophical understandings had existed from time immemorial — in the same sense that Goddess-centered Gaelic myth, folk stories and wealth of language have existed from time immemorial and constitute a vast molten pool of wonderment from which modern bards such as W.B. Yeats, Dylan Thomas, or James Joyce drew their gold. How much greater must the accumulation have been, how much more intact, to have produced a Sappho. How many others must also have been produced whose work did not survive at all.

Sappho wrote to us from an island, a lavender-flowered island as travelers describe it, one of several that were cultural centers for her Greek world of 600 B.C.E. Like Rhodes, Crete or Samos, Lesbos was an island. But to those of us holding Sappho in our mind's eye as *the* historic example both of Lesbianism and of Lesbian poetry, everything she represents lives on an island. That island is separate from, even though it is central to, all of that ancient, ritualized and mundane life of thriving, gorgeous Greece.

Sappho wrote from an island, an island of obvious natural beauty, grace and apparent safety for women; she speaks of gentle gods and prays to a passionate, helpful Aphrodite. The love bonds established between herself and other women were open, accepted, acknowledged, of obvious social value and esteem. Her phrases concerning the loving of women are bordered by descriptions of rites and appropriate behavior to attract the positive attention of the gods.

What was her world like? Well, for one thing, it loved her. She was as popular in her time and the centuries immediately following as the Beatles have been in ours. Her work would not have survived otherwise, for the actual texts were burnt by the Christians in their zeal to eradicate devil worship; in their eyes she was a devil, but by then the words had travelled so far and been quoted so often that some of the bits and phrases escaped destruction. Coins were minted in her land with her portrait on them. What was her own world like? She left us this:

> Coming down from heaven (?), from the mountaintop,
> Hither to me from Crete to this holy temple, where is your
> delightful grove of apple-trees, and altars smoking with in-
> cense; therein cold water babbles through apple-branches,
> and the whole place is shadowed by roses, and from the
> shimmering leaves the sleep of enchantment comes down;
> therein too a meadow, where horses graze, blossoms with
> spring flowers, and the winds blow gently. . . ; there, Cypris,
> take. . . and pour gracefully into golden cups nectar that is
> mingled with our festivities.[3]

No words even remotely resembling these that depict such a world of grace, beauty and feminine magic have been written since her time. I believed for a long time that Sappho's world sounds so idyllic because she must have been wealthy. Yet no Lesbian of wealth has written anything resembling Sappho's descriptions. In fact, *The Well of Loneliness* came to us from the arms of the English upper class, and it is outrightly ugly in its unhappiness.

And what was the nature of Sappho's wealth? She praised it often enough: love, beauty, grace, flowers, appropriate behavior to attract the gods, lovely clothing, intelligence, tenderness. Her poems are filled with the color purple, the color gold, the sun, flowers, especially the violet and the rose, and altars, deer, groves of trees, and the stories of the gods. Love, she said, is a tale-weaver. Wealthy? We own no kind of money that would buy us Sappho's wealth. In her world, women were central to themselves; they had to have been for her to write as she did. She lived on an island of women, in a company of women, from which she addressed all creation. And oh, how they listened.

It is not as if she did not ever speak of sorrow, or separation.

> . . . *and honestly I wish I were dead. She was leaving me with many tears and she said much and this in particular: 'Oh what bad luck has been ours, Sappho; truly I leave you against my will.' I replied to her thus: 'Go and fare well and remember me, for you know how we cared for you. If not, why then I want to remind you. . . and the good times we had. You put on many wreaths of violets and roses and (crocuses?) together by my side, and round your tender neck you put many woven garlands made from flowers and. . . with much flowery perfume, fit for a queen, you anointed yourself. . . and on soft beds. . . . you would satisfy your longing (for?) tender. . .*
>
> *There was neither. . . nor shrine. . . from which we were absent, no grove. . . nor dance. . . sound. . .* '[4]

It is no perfect, idyllic, trouble-free fantasy world that Sappho describes, nor is it the more ancient peaceful Anatolian goddess-worshipping society unearthed at Catal Huyuk by James Mellaart, where no sign of war existed. The war at Troy marked the beginning of the end of the matriarchal era for Western civilization and had already become the wellspring of literature for Sappho's generation. She compares Helen's love for Paris to her own love for a woman she has known. Already the rich forest of Anatolia had been stripped to make ships for war. Sappho found the beauty of women far lovelier than all the mechanics of conquest. *Some say a host of cavalary, others of the infantry, and others of ships, is the most beautiful thing on the black earth, but I say it is whatsoever one loves*, the poem begins, as a splendid affirmation of her own love for Anactoria *who is not here; I would rather see her lovely walk and the bright sparkle of her face than the Lydians' chariots and armed infantry. . .* [5] Tyrants lived in Sappho's time, and she was exiled during her life.[6] The name of the rule of Lesbos during her time would come to be a word meaning "tyrant."

Nevertheless, plenty remained of womanly powers. According to one writer on the nature of Sappho's times: "The customs of the Aeolians permitted more social and domestic freedom than was common in Greece. Aeolian women were not confined to the harem like Ionians, or subjected to the rigorous discipline of the Spartans. While mixing freely with male society, they were highly educated, and accustomed to express their sentiments. . ."[7] The contribution this made to world culture was enormous, as indicated by this description: "Nowhere in any age of Greek history, or in any part of Hellas, did the love of physical beauty, the sensibility to radiant scenes of nature, the consuming fervor of personal feeling, assume such grand proportions and receive so illustrious an expression as they did in Lesbos."[8] And Sappho wrote not to a tiny group of priestesses, but to the world at large — 26 centuries of it — even though much of her writing concerned something so personal, intimate and, in ensuing centuries so hidden, as the love of women for each other.

What Was Sappho's Island Like?

What was Sappho's island like compared to our modern world? We can certainly tell something from examining the fragments of her work and then doing even a cursory comparison with a contemporary book of poetry by Lesbians. *Lesbian Poetry*, edited by Elly Bulkin and Joan Larkin, is a book containing most of the major themes articulated by the highly politicized, self-conscious movement of Lesbian feminism as it has developed in the United States since 1969, when its first voices were raised in overt, concerted number.[9]

From this comparison, we can tell something of what Sappho's life and times were like by looking in mirror perspective, at what they were *not* like. She did not write of Lesbian love out of a negative comparison with heterosexual love, nor by contrasting its merits with anything else, nor by rationalizations such as the following:

> Men are bad, have mistreated women, sexually molested girls, abandoned and robbed us and *therefore* the bond between women is a desirable one — and we will be the height of tender, helpful rescuing of each other. . .

nor is Sappho's work bordered by circumstance:

> Here we are consigned together in this boarding school, jail, convent, military barracks, where it has been made as difficult as possible for us to become lovers. . .

nor is it bordered by walls of fear:

> I would love you gladly if I didn't know we would be punished for it; or I love you in spite of the punishment we go through for it. . . and here are some of the terrible murderous things that happen to Lesbians in our society, and indeed to all kinds of people in our society. . .

nor is it bordered by any sense of restriction:

> I would love you but here I am locked in this castle, family, room, economic strait, social and moral judg-

ment. Or, I do love you and how can I get us out of here — or, here we are, loving each other and trying to get each other out of here.

There is a great deal of lamentation in the work of modern Lesbians, lamentation that Sappho did not speak of in what we know of her work. Indeed, she specified:

> *For it is not right that there should be lamentation in the house of those who serve the Muses. That would not be fitting for us.*[10]

No Lesbian writer that I know of since Sappho (and I'm speaking particularly of Western literature) has written from a context that does not include some form of these strictures and suppressions. Most have hidden their Lesbianism altogether to prevent their work from being destroyed or completely neglected. Emily Dickinson's manuscripts came within a hair's breath of destruction because she allowed so much Lesbian content to stay in them. Sappho's work indicated none of the restrictions, lack of safety, fear of reprisal by husband, police or other patriarchal institution. Her world was not patriarchal.

After the patriarchal change recorded in Homer's account of the war at Troy, the change from a female-centered to a male-centered public world deepened. Sappho's world and the female-bonding that had sustained it nearly disappeared. The new world was masculine in its orientation, and became gradually much more materially centered. Her gods were replaced by one god, and then by no god. Her work was destroyed except for fragments quoted in the work of male writers acknowledging her tremendous influence on them. A bit more (and the only complete poem) was found only recently at the turn of the century, on papyrus wrapped around a body from ancient Egypt. During the intervening centuries, the island of women as a central mind in a culture, sank like Atlantis, and went out of history.

Or not quite out of history. For I take the apple that Sappho said reddened on the topmost branch, and was overlooked by the pickers — no, not so much overlooked as that they could not reach it — I take that apple to mean "female powers." I take it to mean the centrality of women to themselves, to each other and to their society. That apple remained, intact, safe from colonization and suppression, on the topmost branch, and in the fragmented history of a Lesbian poet and her underground descendants.

Poetry repeats and recreates the ceremonial myths which give human lives their meaning beyond the simple worm-like functions, eat, shit, move, reproduce, die, make good soil. Given a ceremonial story, we connect to a group; we connect to a time; we connect to a universe that has a place for us. We *mean*, and our meanings activate us. In the absence of such stories, we not only fall out of public life, we fall out of history, and out of the apple tree. We also fall out of mythic time, out of recognized, central social value. We fall out of poetry except as the objects of it, and as the underlying developers of it, "Muses." Without our names and stories of who we are, we fall out of meaning into a kind of slavery, a no-world, a no-place of worms without even a worm's grace.

What the burning of Sappho's work, and the work of all the ancient women, and indeed more recently the burning of a large number of European women themselves, what all this destruction meant is that women in the West fell out of our own story. We fell, as Lucifer and Diana and paganism and the Fairy people and the whole Old Religion of Europe fell, and then we went to sleep. We fell into a sleep in the middle of our own story. The island that had sustained the core of our knowledge all but sank. Miraculously, the Island of Lesbos was sustained in little fragments; of the Lesbian Poet, barely nine hundred scattered phrases and lines from what had been more than Nine Volumes of 9,000 lines survived, but these were enough to form the memory of a tradition.

This tradition could be called the musings from a House of Women,[11] a female tradition that must once have been mammoth and highly developed. This central house, or island of feminine thought, was not isolated from its society, not underground or veiled. Rather it influenced the world at large, was called upon to do so as is a college or the Supreme Court or any modern institution of intelligence, artfulness and responsibility.

Sappho, addressing another woman, precisely describes what happens when women are disconnected from the house of their Muses. In this poem the house of the Muses is called "Pieria," which is the name of their birthplace in Macedonia. The fruits of this house — art, intelligence, science, music, mathematics, poetry, story — she calls the "roses of Pieria." Women disconnected from this house will be lost to memory, Sappho says; truly a fate worse than mere personal death. It is cultural and spiritual death. Nor, she adds, will such disinherited women return from death in spirit-form,

> *But when you die you will lie there, and afterwards there will never be any recollection of you or any longing for you since you have no share in the roses of Pieria; unseen in the house of Hades also, flown from our midst, you will go to and fro among the shadowy corpses.*[12]

From an Island to a Cloister

After the fall from public power of the women's house, the very names it must have had in the older societies were forbidden and forgotten, and the possibility of the essential female bond, of *Lesbian* love, became a taboo subject. In the interest of forcing the total break with the homosexual, woman-centered, multi-godded, pagan past, literacy itself was forbidden for centuries to all women and most men.

The world of Western women as a community with a center, a public mind, a house of our own, became incorporated over the centuries gradually into the institution of the Christian church, and then cloistered. Sporadic unions of women, the bonding of women in love and in the sharing of intellect, were formed, broken apart and reformed, were split apart and outlawed within the church. Around 1200 A.D., women were thrown very thoroughly out of their power, which had been considerable, within the hierarchy of the church. Before the purge disallowing them to administer sacraments, there were nearly as many women abbots in Europe as there were men. A medieval poem has remained, written from "one religious woman to another," according to John Boswell in his book *Christianity, Social Tolerance and Homosexuality*. It is a lament to lost, almost eternally lost, love. The name of the writer, A., is unknown.

To G., her singular rose
From A. — the bonds of precious love.
What is my strength, that I should bear it,
That I should have patience in your absence?
Is my strength the strength of stones,
That I should await your return?
I, who grieve ceaselessly day and night
Like someone who has lost a hand or a foot?
Everything pleasant and delightful
Without you seems like mud underfoot.
I shed tears as I used to smile,
And my heart is never glad.
When I recall the kisses you gave me
And how with tender words you caressed my little breasts,
I want to die
Because I cannot see you. . .

For no one has been born into the world
So lovely and full of grace,
Or who so honestly
And with such deep affection loves me.
I shall therefore not cease to grieve
Until I deserve to see you again.
Well has a wise man said that it is a great sorrow
For a man to be without that

Without which he cannot live.
As long as the world stands
You shall never be removed from the core of my being.
What more can I say?
Come home, sweet love!
Prolong your trip no longer;
Know that I can bear your absence no longer.
Farewell.
Remember me.[13]

For centuries we have been without the independent institutions, the Islands of Lesbos, the Houses of the Muses and whatever their equivalents are in different ages and cultures — the midwife and market women guilds, the priestess schools, the art-letters-and-science colleges of women, the divinatory and healing societies, all the variety of forms the center of female will and intelligence has structured itself into in order to influence, guide and lead society. Possessing such places, and such centrality to the people of their societies as Sappho had on Lesbos, is exactly what enables women to freely choose who they will or will not bond with. In their absence, Lesbianism has had at best a marginal, flimsy existence. And the apple of public, collective feminine power has hung in a secret tree, waiting.

In the absence of a Women's House or Island of free gathering, women became split from each other, from their mothers and sisters, and from themselves; the sexual bond between women went underground, became lamented, longed for. Besides the cloister, which has been for most centuries a strictly regulated, anti-Lesbian place, the other institution where women were gathered into one place was known as the harem in some cultures, the brothel and whorehouse in others. There, in groups where they are kept with their powers contained as symbols and toys of love for men, the women have bonded. But it is a sad love, it is the love women have for each other when they are in jail. The following poem is from China, written in the 19th century by one courtesan addressing another, and like many another example of modern poetry written by Lesbians addressing the women they love, the courtesan poem is a "rescue" fantasy.

Since the brothel has replaced the sacred grove, the island of the centrality of women has become a confinement. In the poem one of the lovers sings a sad song, a song of the memory of "another place," south of the river — and her lover longs to be able to take her away, to escape with her — to some place, a place that has no name, since it has no existence, or rather, it has no existence because it has no name.

For the Courtesan Ch'ing Lin
To the tune "The Love of the Immortals"
by Wu Tsao

On your slender body
Your jade and coral girdle ornaments chime
Like those of a celestial companion
Come from the Green Jade City of Heaven.
One smile from you when we meet,
And I become speechless and forget every word.
For too long you have gathered flowers,
And leaned against the bamboos,
Your green sleeves growing cold,
In your deserted valley:
I can visualize you all alone,
A girl harboring her cryptic thoughts.

You glow like a perfumed lamp
In the gathering shadows.
We play wine games
And recite each other's poems.
Then you sing "Remembering South of the River"
With its heart breaking verses. Then
We paint each other's beautiful eyebrows.
I want to possess you completely —
Your jade body

And your promised heart.
It is Spring.
Vast mists cover the Five Lakes.
My dear, let me buy a red painted boat
And carry you away.[14]

In the last couple of centuries a new institution where girls and women are sometimes gathered together into one place has developed. It is the boarding school, where they have no autonomy, although they do at times have each other's attention and company. But boarding school, where girls are taken raw from the countryside or from newly colonized areas, breaks them apart from each other and from the "home" culture still further. Themes developing from this institution sometimes include the Lesbian matron as a villainous, hurtful character who rejects and punishes her charges in her role as guardian of the values of the state. Where the themes are of love, the love becomes riddled with the hopelessness and romantic pain indigenous to the colonized. They suffer, and they mourn their love and their loss of it. A novel by Lesbian poet Paula Gunn Allen chronicles this loss in a contemporary scene involving girls in a boarding school in New Mexico, some of whose foremothers were Indians. She has been detailing the bleak sterility of the school:

> She remembered the two sisters who, for a brief time did not look half dead. Sister Mary Grace and Sister Claire. . . Sister Mary Grace and one of the other boarders were playing the piano. Sister Claire had rolled up the sleeves of her habit, pinned the long veil back, decorously, as they often did when they were going to scrub the floor, instead she began to dance. She grabbed one of the girls and began to whirl her around. Sister Mary Grace turned to watch. The tall, heavy girl and the tiny, delicate nun danced and laughed with delight. The girl playing the piano struck up another tune. A polka. The girl dancing with Sister

Claire went spinning off to sprawl, laughing, on a chair next to Ephanie. They crowed with delight. Sister Claire danced up to Sister Mary Grace. She drew Sister Mary Grace to her feet. She pulled her out onto the floor. They began to dance, laughing, giggling, like girls. Their faces growing rosy and gleaming from sweat and exertion. They danced the polka and laughed.

About a week later, Sister Claire was gone. Sent to another school. Or back to the mother house, the place where they were trained and where they lived when they retired. The girls talked about it in whispers. They eyed Sister Mary Grace. Whose face was heavy and dull with grief. Or with something that was not joy. They knew, sort of, what had happened. They were subdued. All of them. No one laughed or danced much the rest of the year. Sister Claire had been sent away and Sister Mary Grace must have wept.

The girls said, they must have been in love. And nodded to each other. And whispered. No one said anything about it being wrong. Ephanie thought now, all these years later, how glad they had all been that someone there was able to love. To laugh and shine and work and play and dance. And how very bereft they all felt when that love was sent away.[15]

From the island in the center of the mind of the Ancient World, the bond between women had retreated, first to the cloister and harem, then to the boarding school, and finally to the spinster's spare bedroom by Emily Dickinson's time in the second half of the nineteenth centry.

The moon has set and the Pleiades, Sappho wrote, *it is midnight, and time goes by, and I lie alone."*[16]

But Sappho never lay so alone as Emily Dickinson lay with her solitary heart in her solitary bed in her solitary room in Amherst, Massachusetts at the end of the Victorian age.[17] Child of a strict Calvinist father who discouraged her poetic thinking, and of a mother who apparently neglected to pay attention to her, Emily fell in love with women she could never go and live with, could not gather in a cloister with, was not closed in a boarding school with, could not ever hold close to her in her narrow and embarrassed bed. Her room became her island of women, where she carried on a one-woman dialogue with the lovers she could not actually gather into her life, and carried on a rousing, introspective one-woman dialogue with death and with the Calvinist god. She said of her room, "Here's freedom."

Adrienne Rich defined Dickinson as a great psychologist in her essay, "Vesuvius at Home: The Power of Emily Dickinson," saying:

> Dickinson is *the* American poet whose work consisted in exploring states of psychic extremity. For a long time, as we have seen, this fact was obscured by the kinds of selections made from her work by timid if well-meaning editors. In fact, Dickinson was a great psychologist, and like every great psychologist, she began with the material she had at hand: herself. She had to possess the courage to enter, through language, states which most people deny or veil with silence.[18]

The basis of Dickinson's extreme isolation was economic as well as social; her father kept her at home as his companion, saw no reason to give her a single penny, and allowed her no traveling even to see a doctor. This situation was typical for white women of the middle classes in the nineteenth century. Several of her physical needs were taken care of, but she was always on a leash. Her mind was not recognized, and neither was her body.

From the content of her letters it is clear that she loved the woman who lived in the house adjoining her father's, her sister-in-law, Susan Gilbert Dickinson. This love and these letters contained expressions of a physical passion that went far beyond even the highly romantic content of correspondence between women in that day. Apparently, at one time, this love was reciprocated.

"Susie, will you indeed come home next Saturday, and be my own again, and kiss me as you used to?" The erotic content of Emily's letters to Susan Dickinson was cut from earlier publications, and has been re-membered by Lillian Faderman in *Surpassing The Love of Men*.[19] Emily loved Sue — who withdrew from her — all her life.

According to biographer Rebecca Patterson in *The Riddle of Emily Dickinson*,[20] a second woman Emily fell in love with when she was twenty eight was Kate Scott, who probably made an amorous offer that Emily was in no position to accept. Highly adventurous and lively, Kate managed to travel by marrying husbands who required her nursing skills and companionship, visiting health spas located in Europe. After seeing two of them into the grave, she inherited money that was hers alone, years after being attracted to, and losing, Emily.

The first thing that Kate, who nicknamed herself "Tommy" and even more dykishly "Thomas," did with her middle-aged financial independence was to take a female lover, a young woman to whom she was companion and teacher. A surviving diary reveals the highly personal information that Kate gave the young woman a gold ring as token of her love, and that they nicknamed each other Mr. and Mrs. Pump. They considered themselves married, in other words. Kate was the "Mr." to her woman lover.[21] All this happened years after Kate Scott went to Amherst and wooed the young Dickinson for a two-year period, then apparently decided the love was hopeless and broke it off (an event Emily seems to have taken as a major theme of heartbreak, of desire and loss, in her work). The summer after Kate's letter rejecting any hope of their continuing and impossible love, Emily wrote of two women who had married one summer:

> Ourselves were wed one summer — dear —
> Your Vision — was in June —
> And when Your little Lifetime failed,
> I wearied — too — of mine —

And overtaken in the Dark —
Where You had put me down —
By Some one carrying a Light —
I — too — received the Sign.

'Tis true — Our Futures different lay —
Your Cottage — faced the sun —
While Oceans — and the North did play —
On every side of mine

'Tis true, Your Garden led the Bloom,
For mine — in Frosts — was sown —
And yet, one Summer, we were Queens —
But You — were crowned in June — [22]

Dickinson, lacking a common language with which to describe her love for other women and her own dykely qualities, made up one of her own in her poetry. Two women together were "queens." She spoke of herself as an "earl" and as having had a "boyhood." How did Kate want her to be, she wrote during the height of their passion in the late 1850's; did Kate want her to be a queen or a page? Tall or short? She, Emily, would be anything, as long as it suited Kate. But the match did not suit Kate. She did not choose to stay in Amherst — and how could she have, where would she have lived? Nor did she persuade Emily to come away with her. How could she have? Where would they have gone with no money? They would not have survived a week. Yet, they played hopeful come here — go away with each other for as long as two years.

Split from the women she loved, Dickinson was split away from herself, a state of mental division she acted out by refusing to sit in the same room with visitors when they came to see her. Dressed perpetually in white like the ghost she thought of herself as being, Dickinson sat in a separate room and spoke to her guests through a half-closed door. Her rage is really evident in this eccentricity. If she could not come into the room as who she was and who she wanted to be, well then, she wouldn't come into it at all.

The love she had wanted, and which represented appreciation, intellectual companionship, a whole world blooming before her, that love had come and offered itself to her when she was without the means and the social support to accept; it had been given to her "without the Suit, Riches and Name and Realm," as she wrote in 1874:

> Frigid and sweet Her parting Face—
> Frigid and fleet my Feet—
> Alien and vain whatever Clime
> Acrid whatever Fate.
>
> Given to me without the Suit
> Riches and Name and Realm—
> Who was She to withhold from me
> Hemisphere and Home?[23]

"Hemisphere and home" could not be hers in this life. From the island of her female mind and isolation, Dickinson wrote repeatedly of death as a possibly happy place, a place where she could be reunited with her love, and with herself, a place where she could find her name:

> The Things that Death will buy
>   Are Room —
> Escape from Circumstances —
> And a Name —[24]

For Dickinson, writing from inside the island of her head, death constituted her only hope that herself and her "flower," by which I believe she meant her sexual, intelligent, worldly, womanly being, could be reunited. Death was the place where reunion with her own womanly powers and love could take place:

> Here, where the Daisies fit my Head
> 'Tis easiest to lie
> And every Grass that plays outside
> Is sorry, some, for me.

Where I am not afraid to go
I may confide my Flower—
Who was not Enemy of Me
Will gentle be, to Her.

Nor separate, Herself and Me
By Distances become—
A single Bloom we constitute
Departed, or at Home— [25]

She spoke for nearly all women of the Victorian age, since she simply represented a more extreme form of many of their lives, which were in every way restricted. Dickinson articulated the most extreme fragmentation Lesbian poets have undergone.

Lacking a language to speak for the special passion she felt and could not satisfy, she created an internal panorama of the mind and the emotions, of our connections to the elemental ways of being and perceiving; lacking a language specific to her own life, she created one that would be of fascination and use to her society for generations to come.

Coming Out of the Cloister with a Cigar

From the room alone, from the isolate, strictured life of the nineteenth century, Lesbians and Lesbian poetry turned a corner, coming out of the Victorian age with cigar smoking Amy Lowell for a leader. Her upper class literary family indulged her as the youngest child, allowed her tomboy childhood, supported her poetry and accepted her eccentric dyke adulthood. Her long-time female marriage to actress Ada Dwyer Russell (nicknamed "Peter"), and her own robust dykeliness were public knowledge. Much of her poetry was overtly Lesbian, and perhaps more importantly, she saw the world as female and herself as its lover:

The Wheel of the Sun

I beg you
Hide your face from me.
Draw the tissue of your head-gear
Over your eyes.
For I am blinded by your beauty,
And my heart is strained,
And aches,
Before you.

In the street,
You spread a brightness where you walk,
And I see your lifting silks
And rejoice:
But I cannot look up to your face.
You melt my strength,
And set my knees to trembling.
Shadow yourself that I may love you,
For now it is too great a pain.[26]

Many of her lines of love to a female world are overtly Lesbian, as
in:

And this paper is dull, crisp, smooth
virgin of loveliness
Beneath my hand.[27]

Given the special role the hand plays in Lesbian love making,
this passage is especially erotic — for Lesbians. She felt protective
in her role as a lover, saying in "A Shower,"

How I love it!
And the touch of you upon my arm
As you press against me that my umbrella
May cover you.[28]

Lowell's poetry, and most especially her love poetry, does not take place in a cloister or a tiny room in one corner of her father's house. Her settings are most often a garden or the countryside. The garden is still a protected place, but at least it is outdoors, in the open, and best of all the female beloved is present in the flesh, walking beside her, loving her. Nowhere in Lowell's work is the beloved a rejecting lost heartbreaker, longed for in later life, as the beloved females are in Dickinson's lines. The poems to Ada and to the womanly world are not the memory of lost love, not the longing of unrequited and helpless adolescence, not the desire and longing for escape together from an unbearable life. Though Lowell does perceive the city as a threatening place in "The Taxi," it is still in the context of love as a haven:

. . . Streets coming fast
One after the other,
Wedge you away from me,
And the lamps of the city prick my eyes
So that I can no longer see your face.
Why should I leave you,
To wound myself on the sharp edges of the night?[29]

However, most of her love poems are not this urban; they use imagery of flowers, of which she knew a great deal, having been born into an estate that was rich with landscape and having a lifetime love of gardening. "Ah, Dear, I love you," she simply ends one poetic description of two lovers who are flowers, one purple, one crimson.[30] In "Reflections," she sees in the beloved's eyes much more than a garden, she sees a whole world of grace and beauty, and a woman's hand reaching in to grasp it:

Reflections

When I looked into your eyes
I saw a garden
With peonies, and tinkling pagodas

And round-arched bridges
Over still lakes.
A woman sat beside the water
In a rain-blue, silken garment.
She reached through the water
To pluck the crimson peonies
Beneath the surface,
But as she grasped the stems,
They jarred and broke into white-green ripples;
And as she drew out her hand,
The water-drops dripping from it
Stained her rain-blue dress like tears.[31]

But that world does not exist, and the image breaks, and the poem ends with wistful sorrow. Lowell's work was heavily criticized for its Lesbian content during the 1920's, and there is no hint of her Lesbianism in the work chosen for anthologizing. Had she not smoked a cigar and had the habit of sitting with her feet on the desk, I would not have spotted and recognized her as a dyke in my own isolated early days. Born the same year as Gertrude Stein, she died much earlier, living in fear, apparently, that she would outlive her lover Ada Russell. She died in 1923 at the age of 49, having set the stage through her work with the Imagist Movement for her contemporary, H.D., who was just launching her own work in 1923, as also was Lowell's other natural contemporary, Gertrude Stein.

As Lowell did for Ada Russell, Stein made certain her lifetime female lover is present in her work. In her photographs as well as in the texts of her writing, Alice B. Toklas is included. She is present as the lover, even publicly so, tucked inside Stein's carefully coded verbal disguises.

For all of the tremendous range of her mind, Stein's settings rarely leave the interior of a house, usually taking place in one room; mundane objects of a room are given the same value in her sentences as persons, and indeed so are the verbs, adjectives, articles and conjunctions. Exiles from a still brawling, anti-intellectual Western America, Stein and Toklas created their own little island in Paris, with a coterie of Lesbian friends, and with a peculiarly French form of cloister: the literary and artistic salon. The two Jewish women brought into their self-defined salon world every artist and writer of any importance within their sphere of influence, all men. But though she drew stimulation from men, sat among them in her house, taught them and influenced them, Stein's work centered almost entirely on women, and — basic to this — on solving the problems of expressing and naming a Lesbian life in a world that forbade doing so.

Her first novel, *Q.E.D.* (abbreviation for the Latin phrase meaning "things as they are") is about three young Lesbians involved in a love triangle. The solution of the triangle situation is the book's focal point, rather than the subject of Lesbianism and its relation to the external world. The Lesbianism, in fact, is so taken for granted in the text that she achieved what has been a goal for Lesbian prose writers who have succeeded her: writing a Lesbian novel in which the characters just "happen" to be Lesbian. Small wonder that in an era that saw *The Well of Loneliness*[32] become widely known with its wringing plea for "acceptance" for the terrible aberration, Stein's simple novel of three lovers was so unpublishable that she shelved it for the duration of her life. "Things as they are," was not a marketable commodity even among literary folk in her day (nor are they now). She believed that the book would reach publication within a decade or so of her death in 1946. But not until 1973 was it possible to get more than an underground photocopied version of *Q.E.D.*. (I seem to recall having such a ms. pass through my hands, in 1970 or 1971.) After putting away as unpublishable such overt reference to the facts of her own life, Stein developed a style that could include this personal content without evoking the taboo.

Richard Kostelanetz says in his introduction to *The Yale Gertrude Stein*, a collection published in 1983, "In *Tender Buttons*, which was begun in 1911 and finished the following year, her aim was the creation of texts that described a thing without mentioning it by name."[33] She surrounded the subject without ever naming it. And in doing so, she found a solution to that central problem of her own forbidden existence — for how can a creative writer write without having the free use of her own life to do it with? In solving that huge problem, by surrounding the subject of Lesbianism and of her love and the rich, lively life she had with Alice Toklas without ever naming them, she did the same for all her ideas; she surrounded all of them with provocative verbal structures without ever naming them. In so doing she began to teach the entire English speaking world some new tools with which to think — to think without using names.

Stein disseminated the essence of the forbidden — and untouchable — Lesbian apple into the homey atmosphere of her work in the most subtle of ways, most of which have barely been decoded in our era. Meanwhile, her contemporary H.D. was placing it, and the centrality of women's power, into some very external contexts. Like Stein, H.D. is a giant twentieth century poet. (Amy Lowell is a door opener, by contrast, having died too soon to develop the huge body of work necessary for her to reach their stature.) H.D. developed the ancient metaphor of the orchard as a sacred place. She described the orchard not just as a secular garden with some wishful Venus statues, as Lowell did, but as a real grove of real female power.

What has been best known of H.D.'s work is its thinnest, earliest parts featuring the spareness of clean imagery sought by a generation of American poets as they broke with the nineteenth century. "Imagist" was the tag for what they were doing, and H.D. was considered the best. Yet, pretty as "whirl up, sea" is as an image, it is nothing, a puff of air, compared to the full-bodied bulk of H.D.'s work as it grew to fruition in the context of her forty year long Lesbian marriage to the woman Bryher, which began in 1919.

Raised a Moravian in Pennsylvania (born in Bethlehem), H.D. watched her first marriage, to Richard Aldington, deteriorate as the First World War gradually took his attention from her world of poetry and beauty, to the mechanized destruction that consumed two generations of European, American and Asian men. Pregnant, alone, devastated by despair, she was literally rescued by young Bryher, daughter of a shipping magnate. Bryher took her to the Greek Islands where she recovered, though she was to suffer several more breakdowns in her life. Her work, more specifically descended from Sappho's than that of the other Lesbian poets under discussion, centered on defining the essential female mythos for our time. She found the most essential image in Helen, another great beauty who endured another Great War. For H.D. the "apple," or "island" of female centrality was not Lesbianism itself, but it was her Lesbian relationship that enabled her to see her society and the relation of Woman to it.

Islands were recurrent in her relationship with Bryher and to her own art; it was to an island Bryher took her to have her child, a daughter, Perdita. H.D.'s frame of reference was "island" — Greece (and then ancient Egypt), especially; in Helen she constructed an image of hiding out from the war on a special, white island. H.D. used classical mythology and Hermetic philosophy as a code of her own in which to lay down a philosophical exploration of female power in a masculine world. Bryher, too, used "island" to describe who she was; she named herself for an island off Scotland: Bryher. And the two of them together, even when sometimes involved triangularly with a man, constituted a little island of cultivation and protection for their literary work.

Although overtly Lesbian sexual imagery is more sparse in H.D.'s work than it is in Lowell's, near the end of her writing life she wrote these supreme erotic Lesbian lines:

> . . . you say there is dried fruit
>
> in the amphora and the wine-jars,
> but I would wander in the Elysian-fields
> and find the Tree for myself — for myself —

with a special low down-sweeping burdened bough,
low enough so that I could kneel
and savor the fragrance of the cleft fruit

on the branch, intoxicant;
I would be intoxicated with the scent of fruit,
O, holy apple, O, ripe ecstasy[34]

The hot richness of that particular apple did not reach far enough to touch my young life, even though H.D. was writing those words in 1959, the year I went to live with my first lover. We knew nothing of Lesbian poets in the past — except Sappho — and as two lovers we constituted an "island" as well, one of extreme secrecy and isolation. Yet only ten years later, in 1969, I would write a set of poems that set an overtly Lesbian figure in a context of other women. "Carol in the park, chewing on straws" is one of seven portraits in *The Common Woman Poems*. In this poem, the woman is definitely out of the garden and out of her father's house; she is also free of coded language and covert messages. In the poem she is squarely located in a public park, not passing through, but staying there in the open, chewing on straws, contemplating her life. She has a woman lover with whom she lives, and the poem makes it clear that they keep this a secret from others by lying about it. The poem reveals the secret of their life together, and sets them into a context with other "common" women, women who also have secrets and dire needs of one kind or another, that are also being made public. The Lesbian is set into a context of other women, regular, ordinary American women. She is "cloistered" only by virtue of the closet of secrecy that cuts her off from other people, and so her life is an unknown thing being revealed. She dreams:

On weekends, she dreams of becoming a tree;
a tree that dreams it is ground up
and sent to the paper factory, where it

lies helpless in sheets, until it dreams
of becoming a paper airplane and rises
on its own current; where it turns into a
bird, a great coasting bird that dreams of becoming
more free, even, than that — a feather, finally, or
a piece of air with lightning in it.[35]

She is angry energy, and a thunderstorm. By 1971 Carol in the
park with her woman lover has been "decloistered" altogether; she
now lives, along with a poem titled "A History of Lesbianism," in
a bold little blue book called *Edward the Dyke and Other Poems*, a
title chosen precisely for its use of the magical underground taboo
word. This was not the first time the word "Lesbian" had appeared
in poetry, but probably no poetry book ever had "dyke" in it.

Though my voice was the first of the poets considered in this
particular lineage of lines and images to use and publish overtly
Gay terminology and experience,[36] I was followed rapidly by Black
activist Pat Parker. We worked as a team doing readings for years.
We heard Audre Lorde read her work on the West Coast, and she
had visited both of us, spending long hours especially talking to
Pat Parker. Soon, Lorde came all the way out of the closet in her
work and public image. This must have been a particularly terror-
ridden passage given the obvious threat that as Black Lesbians
they could lose the support of the Black community and be left to
drift alone in a racist and homophobic world. Lorde had already
established her poetic reputation, growing out of the beatnik roots
of her development (with her early co-heart in poetry, Diane
DiPrima) into her own highly individual mythic-lyric-political
voice, within the context of the Black political and cultural movements of the 1960's. She had published *First Cities* and *Cables To
Rage* by 1970.

Adrienne Rich had achieved recognition among mainstream
poetic audiences as early as publication of her first book, *A Change
of Worlds*, in 1953. She shifted voices as the feminist and Lesbian/
feminist ideology and activism geared up in the early Seventies,
infusing her careful, socially analytical poetry with compelling

feminism, an internal, close-in voice. She quickly drew the attention of a great many women with her 1973 volume, *Diving Into The Wreck*. She then stepped firmly onto an overtly Lesbian poetic literary path with *Twenty One Love Poems*, written between 1974 and 1976, and *The Dream of a Common Language*, published in 1978.

Olga Broumas surfaced with five Lesbian love poems, *Caritas*, in 1976, and *Beginning with O* in 1977, chosen for the Yale series of younger poets. Earlier, in 1975, she had written "Twelve Aspects of God" in conjunction with twelve oil paintings by artist Sandra McKee, exhibited at a gallery in Eugene, Oregon. She took the stage as a Lesbian poet from the beginning of her public presentations of her art. The erotic/sacred content of her work, as well as her classical frame of reference (which as a native of Greece she is surely entitled to, if anyone is), places her directly in a line with Sappho.

Paula Gunn Allen is another poet who, like Lorde and Rich had already fixed a place for herself in a different sphere, in her case the sphere of burgeoning American Indian poetry, literature and criticism. Having participated in the Bay Area poetic community since the early Sixties, as well as being heavily published in academic circles, she gained attention in the Lesbian feminist community dramatically in 1981, with her poem "Beloved Women" and the accompanying essay "Beloved Women: Lesbians in American Indian Cultures."[37] Her work was both startling and exciting in that it acknowledged for the first time a special office of Lesbianism held among American Indian tribes in former times.

The overlapping work of these five writers articulate the major themes and definitions of Lesbian poetry as it developed from 1969 into the 1980's.[38]

The first thing we did was find a new setting. Beyond the city park of Carol with her contemplative straws, the city itself became the new location for the poems of Lesbian poets, even while urban life is often seen as a hostile environment full of danger, male technology, violence, dirt and opposition to the Lesbian bond. The new "island" of Lesbianism includes acceptance, even positive use of, the outcast state from which the new Lesbians will build a "Lesbian Nation." To be sure, we have not lost our gardens. My set of poems, "Confrontations with the Devil in the Form of Love" is completely dependent on the presence of apple trees, though it is otherwise urban in reference. But in recent Lesbian poetry, the garden is no longer the major place, in fact it may have become a paltry, undersized container for larger ambitions. Audre Lorde describes going hand in hand with her lover into her backyard garden after a winter of difficulty in a poem called "Walking Our Boundaries:"

> . . . The sun is watery warm
> our voices
> seem too loud for this small yard
> too tentative for women
> so in love
> the siding has come loose in spots
> our footsteps hold this place
> together
> as our place
> our joint decisions make the possible
> whole. . . [39]

She clearly states that the *place* itself is formed by their Lesbian marriage, which has outgrown itself.

A Crossing to a Heart-Shaped Place

During this time, Lesbians are leaving cloister, isolate rooms, and safely enclosed gardens to cross into public life. It is during the period from 1973 to 1977 that some of the poets write of a "crossing" in which a pair of Lesbians make a perilous modern urban journey in which they have an insight about their situation with respect to the rest of the world. The most developed of these is my own "A Woman is Talking to Death," written in February of 1973 and published a year later.

This crossing takes place on the Bay Bridge, on which the two Lesbians witness a motorcycle accident. A very careless young white man is killed in this accident, and the white policemen and court system blame the death upon the Black driver. The poem is a series of meditations on both modern urban and historical situations, especially centering on the position of women, but with cross-reference to people of color in American society, among many other things. The poem confronts and challenges the Christian mythic system of celebrating the heroism of martyred white men, by revealing it as arrogant, as wasteful, and as intolerably harmful to the people of the society who don't fit that definition. The poem's solution is that the women (and their "lovers") will not continue to be victimized by the myth of the hero, or male or white supremacy, of modern industrialization, or "death" as the antagonist is called in the poem. "Real loving" is that decision to no longer agree to victimization. In fact, the poem ends, the women and those who can connect to them will go somewhere else, out of the myth; they will stop working for it, and go to be with each other and to prepare the way for a different world. And the myth of death shall be left behind, and shall be "poor."

In the poem, the drastic intercultural and intergender oppressions which are everywhere manifest and in which all of us are completely enmeshed, are offset only by a delicate refrain: "My lover's teeth are white geese / flying above me / my lover's muscles are rope ladders / under my hands." The image conjures a ship's sails and a ship's ladders, not a modern ship but an old fashioned vessel, perhaps going to an ancient land. The two lovers together, now one flying above and now the other, constitute the ship. They are taking each other someplace. Geese, incidently, is another word for Gay, as in the phrase, "Gay as a goose."[40]

Olga Broumas has a crossing poem, published in 1977 in her first book *Beginning with O*. Broumas' awakening of Sleeping

Beauty, of the slumbering goddess within us waking to the memory of a woman's love on her lips, is set in the city, like most of Rich's "Twenty One Love Poems" and all but the refrain of "A Woman is Talking to Death."

> City-center, mid-
> traffic, I
> wake to your public kiss. Your name
> is Judith, your kiss a sign
>
> to the shocked pedestrians, gathered
> beneath the light that means
> stop
> in our culture
> where red is a warning, and men
> threaten each other with final violence: *I will drink*
> *your blood.* Your kiss
> is for them
>
> a sign of betrayal, your red
> lips suspect, unspeakable
> liberties as
> we cross the street, kissing
> against the light, singing, *This*
> *is the woman I woke from sleep, the woman that woke*
> *me sleeping.*[41]

In a place that is located in the very center of the city, the Lesbians are kissing each other awake with a public kiss, are accepting an outcast status, are in fact holding each other and kissing against the light on purpose. Their outcast status is the new island from which they will view the rest of the world, and comment upon it; and at last the island of women — however uncomfortably — is located out of the tight little rooms, the half-sheltered gardens and the dreamlike orchards of the lover's mind. It does not have to be exotically, toleratedly perched in the rarified air of the upper class with Lowell, nor exiled in the safety of Switzerland with H.D. and

Bryher; now the love is public, is out in the open in America. It is in the world. And as such it is a step in reclaiming the world, for women, and of renaming the stories of being out in the world, this time with women in them. The bridge to the island of ourselves has begun.

The first collection of works by women of color with many of the authors openly identified as Lesbian is titled *This Bridge Called My Back*. For these writers, their own minds and bodies and spirits constitute of necessity the bridge of flesh that crosses from one culture to another, from one world view to another. They are making the crossing from race to race as well as locating a place to be women together. In so doing they hold out promise that all of us will be led to a much larger, fuller, more intricate "island" than anything we could ever imagine as one group alone.

Audre Lorde calls for us to "stop killing / the other / in our-selves / the self that we hate / in others."[42] The bridge to others is herself. The bridge to herself is the bridge to others. In Lorde's work, she is her own bridge, and she calls on Seboulisa, mother of power, to help her with her crossing:

October

Spirits
of the abnormally born
live on in water
of the heroically dead
in the entrails of snake.
Now I span my days like a wild bridge
swaying in place
caught between poems like a vise
I am finishing my piece of this bargain
and how shall I return?

Seboulisa, mother of power
keeper of birds
fat and beautiful

give me the strength of your eyes
to remember
what I have learned
help me to attend with passion
these tasks at my hand for doing.
Carry my heart to some shore
that my feet will not shatter
do not let me pass away
before I have a name
for this tree
under which I am lying.
Do not let me die
still
needing to be stranger.[43]

The call is for a new island, some new shore that does not shatter underfoot, a name — a name for a place that is already happening, as the poet says she is already lying under the tree of it.

Adrienne Rich's "Twenty One Love Poems," written in 1974 after she had read "A Woman Is Talking to Death," contains a crossing. This is a ferry crossing in which two Lesbian lovers are confined in the cabin with the other couples, straight people, newly-weds, representing the most openly expressive form of the heterosexual culture that has been so prohibitive of the homosexual culture. And in the poem the narrator puts her hand on her lover's knee, openly, and has never felt closer to her than at this moment when they can, at last, be public. They can be public because everyone is so seasick no one is going to notice that they are doing this taboo thing. In "Twenty One Love Poems," Rich is calling for a love based in reality, "I told you from the first I wanted daily life, / this island of Manhattan is island enough for me." She wants a Lesbian life that is not exotic, in other words, not in exile, not hidden and not located on a fantasy island, but rather is right there in the contemporary urban island of Manhattan, as a full and public life.

And yet, how to do this? For what is the meaning of it, the *ritual* significance? What is the story we can tell ourselves of our doings that gives our lives meaning? What connects us back to the Roses of the Muses, and to the highest apple that is ourselves? "No one has imagined us," Rich says. And therefore, we have no way of imagining ourselves; until we can, we have no real, meaningful being. In the last of the "Twenty One Love Poems," she locates a new island. "Stonehenge," she says, but not really Stonehenge, rather it is something *like* Stonehenge, a place of the past that is actually waiting for us in the future. It is a special, measured place where she as a woman and as an open Lesbian has chosen to go, to "draw this circle," a circle in which she and her lovers can live, and can envision their lives into a meaningful scheme, a new dream.

What is the Nature of This Dream, This New Island?

"Is my strength the strength of stones, / That I should await your return?" The Medieval Lesbian wrote, seven hundred years ago.[44]

Apparently the strength of stones *is* what is called for, at least as it appears in the imagery of the Lesbian poets of this discussion. In Lorde's words, in "Woman," the new stones are located in a place wherein the "commonest rock / is moonstone and ebony opal / giving milk to all my hungers. . ."[45] She makes clear who the "stones" will be in the "Journeystones I-IX," a set of portraits of women she knows. The stones are each woman and ourselves, and each other *in* ourselves, even in our apparent oppositions of race and class, of moonstone and ebony opal.

Olga Broumas describes three muses casting stones on an earthen platter, "till the salt veins aligned, and she read the cast":

> *Whatever is past*
> *and has come to an end*
> *cannot be brought back by sorrow*[46]

For Paula Gunn Allen, as for the other Lesbian poets, the new island is a psychic place, a shared vision, one especially keenly visualized during the sexual closeness with a lover. The new world to be envisioned is right here, in the everyday life we have in common with all women and ultimately with all people. We will not transform what we perceive as a very limited, one-sided half-civilization. To use words from Rich:

> . . . this still unexcavated hole
> called civilization, this act of translation, this half-world,[47]

cannot be transformed enough by violent revolution, and certainly not by transcendence *from* it, by escape or by constructing a "heaven" in the skies. Rather we will transform it by living in it, while yet holding a second vision, a new dream/vision, in our minds at the same time. In defining the precise dimensions of that dream, by attempting to live it, and by helping each other to see and feel and express it, we will affect the world, by changing its mind.[48]

"Beauty of the moon rests directly on the darkness of the sky," Allen says. By repeatedly placing dark and light images side by side, she is positing a harmonious whole, rather than a set of oppositions. In "Moonstream," Allen describes the interplay of dark and light:

> We walked into the lodge of the moon
> and lay
> at the center of the stones
> that give us light
> you placed your hand deep in shadow hollows
> and the flowers deep in my mooncave
> spilled their perfume over you
> moon woman followed our ways —
> spilling her perfume between my legs
> knees rising in the shadows
> mountain peaks holding moon
> perfectly in shadow framed.[49]

38

Only a one-sided patriarchal mind could separate the brightness of the moon from the dark sky that holds it and makes it possible. The Lesbian at the heart of her mind knows that dark and light are the same thing. To quote H.D., *"l'ile blanche is l'ile noire;"* (the white island is the black island). When we understand this, we can put our broken selves back together. We have already begun to uncover the stones necessary to build another island.

Adrienne Rich, in *The Dream of A Common Language*, locates a new island,

> . . . Not Stonehenge
> simply nor any place but the mind
> casting back to where her solitude,
> shared, could be chosen without loneliness,
> not easily nor without pains to stake out
> the circle, the heavy shadows, the great light.
> I choose to be a figure of that light,
> half-blotted by darkness, something moving
> across that space, the color of stone
> greeting the moon, yet more than stone:
> a woman. I choose to walk here. And to draw this circle.[50]

And she goes on from this to "Transcendental Etude," a poem in which she finds her way to a new rock, a new sense of home and of homesickness:

> . . . Such a composition has nothing to do with eternity,
> the striving for greatness, brilliance—
> only with the musing of a mind
> one with her body, experienced fingers quietly pushing
> dark against bright, silk against roughness,
> pulling the tenets of a life together
> with no mere will to mastery,
> only care for the many-lived, unending
> forms in which she finds herself,
> becoming now the sherd of broken glass
> slicing light in a corner, dangerous

to flesh, now the plentiful, soft leaf
that wrapped round the throbbing finger, soothes the
                              wound;
and now the stone foundation, rockshelf further
forming underneath everything that grows.[51]

The idea of the woman as the earth coupled with the idea of
the earth as an active principle is a turnabout from the stock
stereotypes that the woman, as "wife" and as "mother," as "weeping
Madonna," or the "black goddess black hope black strength- /
black mother" to quote Lorde in "Need: A Choral of Black
Women's Voices,"[52] is a long-suffering rock of stability simply en-
during her unchangeably horrible circumstance. Earth as an actor
with her own mind is a very old tribal idea; she appears in my *She
Who* poems, written in 1972, as a volcano who is a "woman of
strong purpose" and, much more playfully, in the limerick:

She Whose skin is pited with tiny holes
filled them up with microscopic moles,
who multiplied so quickly she was led
to fill them up with prairie dogs instead.[53]

In "a plainsong from an older woman to a younger woman,"
the speaker asks herself to remember:

was I not   ruling
guiding   naming
was I not   brazen
crazy   chosen

even the stones would do my bidding?[54]

Among other things, this is a reference to the ancient story
that women sang the pyramid stones into place with their voices
and a special magical instrument. In this poem the older woman
speaker asserts herself completely, "I am the will," she says, "and
the riverbed." That the riverbed has a will has not been a Western

idea. But it is an idea completely essential to the reclamation by women of our own powers.

The new island is being built of living rocks, as alive as apples, and as quickly as we can uncover them in our own lives:

The land that I grew up on is a rock

From my mother, a rock,
I have learned that rocks give
most of all.
What do rocks do? They hold the
forces of the earth together and
give direction . . .

They are like bone, the rocks. They frame.
They remain. They hold you.
They grind together to make digestible dirt . . .

the center of a rock, particularly
the one we live on,
is molten like a star, the core
is light,
enlightening, giving of
intelligence . . . [55]

In taking the Lesbian — and by extension, every woman — out of the realm of the exotic and placing her in the ordinary and everyday, woman with all her powers becomes central rather than extreme. What she has in common with herself and with other women becomes more important than what she is that is different from men. The new island of centrality, the centrality that is constructed of what is held in common, is of prime importance to the redefining being done by Lesbian poets.

The definition of *place* itself has been central to what we have done. The first overtly Lesbian poem I wrote began, "in the place where / her breasts come together" and continued "in the place where / her legs come together."[56] Those were the most taboo, the most highly charged places forbidden for me to speak of — until then.

The first woman-owned and run bookstore of our current feminist era was named by its Lesbian/feminist founders, "A Woman's Place," the entire phrase being "A Woman's Place Is In the World." They consciously envisioned their bookstore as a place for women to come, alternative to the constriction of the home as well as of the workplace, and of the forbidden, dangerous streets. One of the first Lesbian novels of the 1970's era was *A Place for Us*, the original title of Isabel Miller's *Patience and Sarah*. Even *Rubyfruit Jungle* is making reference to a location; being a takeoff on the term "Blackboard Jungle." It helped push Lesbianism out into the world, a hostile world at times, to be sure, a "jungle" but nevertheless we were perceived, and perceiving ourselves as out of the house, out of confinement. In our lives, we have felt greatly without place, and continually out of place.

Audre Lorde, speaking about the alienation brought about by racism, sexism and the great difficulty of Lesbian parenthood, wrote these wrenching lines in "School Note":

My children play with skulls
and remember
for the embattled
there is no place
that cannot be
home
nor is.[57]

"Home" for Lorde is an embattled place, not certainly in the sense of her own close-knit home — but in the sense of the Black Lesbian poet (and all she represents) out in the world. Apples are not the fruit of choice in Lorde's imagery; she is not writing from a European folk-tradition (as I am and Broumas is, for instance). Solidly based in the area of Manhattan and the modern world of urban Black America, Lorde draws additionally from the Barbadian birthland of both her parents, and also (especially in *The*

Black Unicorn and her novel *Zami*) from West Africa and the Yoruba/Macumba traditions. Her island is real, contemporary, as much as it is historical. It is the Caribbean Island of Grenada, lost to her as a child of immigrants from it, as all our parents' lands are lost to us; lost again and more forcefully (though never permanently) in the degraded invasion of tiny Grenada by the U.S. military in 1983.

The fruits in Lorde's work are fruits that bring women together, bring about the wholeness of spirit necessary for "women's power" to centralize itself. The fruits are tropical, avocados and mangoes mashed tantalizingly and licked from the belly by the (female) lover; spicey nutmeg (Grenada grows nutmeg as a primary crop) is ground like deep unspeakable emotions and thoughts in her mother's mortar, as the adolescent girl poet watches in pain and wonder and desire. The ideal "place" of power in Lorde's work is in the act of female bonding, a tie that does not always happen, and never happens easily. There are no facile answers in her complex imagery.

Again and again the contemporary Lesbian poets have stated the necessity of wholeness and integration as the way to a place, to home, and to the fruit of a new world. The Lesbian poet, through her Gay cultural traditions, through the poetic traditions to which she is heir through her art, and through her experiences as a woman — in some instances as a woman wih an alive ethnic tribal cultural tradition as well — such Lesbian poets have a memory of an island, a world. "A planet," as H.D. called it, as she called Sappho herself, far different from life in this current world. Such Lesbian poets have the understanding that each woman is her own Muse, and in so doing we have found our sense of place with each other.

The nature of *place* is female, that is, the word derived from the female body, from *placenta*, the place where the child is joined to its mother. "Who is your mother?" is the question, according to Paula Gunn Allen, of prime importance to the Pueblo Indian world; location in your mother's house is what gives you your sense of place in the social world.[58] "Location" is a similar idea as placenta, being related to the same root as "lochial," meaning "birthing," as in "lochial blood." The way home for women is the way to ourselves.

When a woman is one with herself, is reunited after being fragmented from the female world, she is also reunited with her sense of place, with *place* itself. And in seeing herself as the Muse, herself as an active principle, she also sees the earth as an active principle. She sees it as a living apple, rather than an inert substance to be manipulated from without, or to render inspiration to "others." When the woman unites with the female in the universe she feels it inside of herself. "What do I have / if not my 2 hands & my apples."[59] I wrote on occasion of losing all my property, and much of my sense of identity. Olga Broumas, in a beautiful poem of a daughter uniting with her mother:

> Like two halves
> of a two-colored apple—red
> with discovery, green with fear—we lay
> . . . Defenseless
> and naked as the day
> I slid from you
> twin voices keening and the cord
> pulsing our common protest, I'm coming back
> back to you
> woman, flesh
> of your woman's flesh, your fairest, most
> faithful mirror,
>   my love
> transversing me like a filament
> wired to the noonday sun.
>
> Receive
> me, Mother.[60]

When a woman unites with the female in the universe she feels it inside of herself, and she perceives its willful powers, as

44

Sappho must also, when she prayed to those powers to aid her in her purposes:

> Let your (graceful form appear) near me (while I pray), lady
> Hera. . . now (be gracious and help me) in accordance with
> that ancient precedent.[61]

Lesbian poetry leads itself to its own foundations, and to this idea: the universe is alive, is a place, and we can unite with it; in fact it is essential that we do so. We can build a place for ourselves in it, so long as we understand the stones to be each other; we can reach our long-held apple, the one Sappho held back on the highest branch for us. This is a profoundly tribal and profoundly feminist and a profoundly poetic and a profoundly Lesbian idea.

Part II

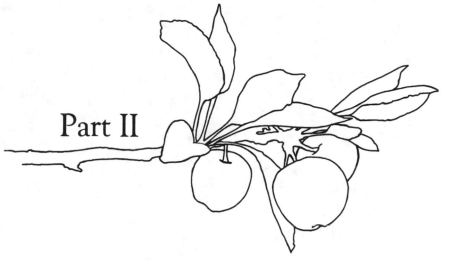

Writing From
A House Of Women

Writing From
A House of Women

And Sappho said this: *Hither now, tender Graces and lovely-haired Muses.*[1] And this: *Stand (before me), if you love me, and spread abroad the grace that is on your eyes.*[2]

Sappho wrote from the base of Lesbianism, of bonded women in an intact culture, who had common understandings, a common mythological framework, a shared religion. She was central to her culture, and even in fragments has been central as a poet in Western culture as it has developed over twenty five centuries.

Once an Alexandrian poet named Meleager referred to Sappho as "little — but all roses." The poet closest in quality to Sappho in the twentieth century, H.D., disagreed not only that she was "little," but also that "roses" was an apt description for the centrality of her position in her own world. In her essay, "The Wise Sappho," H.D. wrote of her as:

> Not roses, but an island, a country, a continent, a planet, a world of emotion, differing entirely from any present day imaginable world of emotion; a world of emotion that could only be imagined by the greatest of her own countrymen in the greatest period of that

country's glamour, who themselves confessed her beyond their reach, beyond their song, not a woman, not a goddess even, but a song or the spirit of a song.

A song, a spirit, a white star that moves across the heaven to mark the end of a world epoch or to presage some coming glory.[3]

Sappho wrote *from* the context of a women's community, or what could be termed a "House of Women," *into* the context of her society at large. As a poet of her whole society she wrote stories illustrative of the doings of the gods, both male and female; she wrote instructions for the appropriate behavior with respect to the gods and to human society; and she wrote wedding songs, as well as the overtly Lesbian love lyrics for which she is so famed and ill-famed, for which her work was burnt and partially submerged. In everything that remains of what she did, she maintained a female-based point of view, a female collective center from which to speak of life and death, of beauty and love in general. She used an internal, subjective voice in an objective, public manner.

Sappho used clear, precise description and example to illustrate her points, drawing from the religious mythology and stories which were well understood as metaphors, as instructions for ordering the universe by the people of her time. So to give example of her love for a certain woman, Anactoria, she drew on the story of Queen Helen:

Some say a host of cavalary, others of infantry, and others of ships, is the most beautiful thing on the black earth, but I say it is whatsoever a person loves. It is perfectly easy to make this understood by everyone: for she who far surpassed mankind in beauty, Helen left her most noble husband and went sailing off to Troy with no thought at all for her child or dear parents, but (love) led her astray. . . lightly. . . (and she?) has reminded me now of Anactoria who is not here; I would rather see her lovely walk and the bright sparkle of her face than the Lydians' chariots and armed infantry. . . impossible to happen. . . mankind. . . but to pray to share. . . unexpectedly.[4]

As Helen loved Paris, so do I love you, Anactoria, she said in a very socialized and external voice. She often used a subjective internal voice as well, and H.D. felt that voice is the one we love most about her:

> The gods, it is true,. . . are mentioned in these poems but at the end, it is for the strange almost petulant little phrases that we value this woman, this cry (against some simple unknown girl) of skirts and ankles we might think unnecessarily petty, yet are pleased in the thinking of it, or else the outbreak against her own intimate companions brings her nearer our own over-sophisticated, nerve-wracked era: "The people I help most are the most unkind," "O you forget me," or "You love someone better," "You are nothing to me," nervous, trivial tirades. Or we have in sweetened mood so simple a phrase "I sing" — not to please any god, goddess, creed or votary of religious rite — I sing not even in abstract contemplation, trance-like, remote from life, to please myself, but says this most delightful and friendly woman, "I sing and I sing beautifully like this, in order to please my friends — my girl friends."[5]

It is this wholeness of itself that has given Sappho's work such value, and so much power as to keep the little scattered phrases vibrant and meaningful. In spite of tremendous opposition, deliberate misinterpretation, branding of her person as a moral degenerate, and the tranformations of society over twenty five hundred years' time, the words speak strong and clear today. She spoke of and to the gods, in her own personal voice, undistanced from them. In so doing, she spoke into the most collective consciousness of her culture without omitting her own personal consciousness. She spoke from a whole way of being, not an alienated, fragmented one; she spoke not as an outcast, but as someone at the very heart and center of her culture and of her times.

Her place was on an island, from what can be imagined as a "House of Women" in the middle of her world. This is a place of far more power than any of the descriptive titles and names modern people have tried to put to what she did. She was, far more than a priestess in a religion of Aphrodite, teacher to daughters of a dying gynarchy, salon-hostess to a bevy of active artists or just a lyre-playing Lesbian with a lot of sexy friends. She wrote from such an integrated female place as we modern women have only begun to imagine.

Even in the sparse fragments that remain, the names of her lovers and cohorts in the group around her are many, and her usual attitude toward them is instructive and descriptive praise:

> I bid you, Abanthis, take (your lyre?) and sing of Gongyla, while desire once again flies around you, the lovely one — for her dress excited you when you saw it; and I rejoice;. . .[6]

> . . . Sardis. . . often turning her thoughts in this direction. . . (she honoured) you as being like a goddess for all to see and took most delight in your song. Now she stands out among Lydian women like the rosy-fingered moon after sunset, surpassing all the stars, and its light spreads alike over the salt sea and the flowery fields; the dew is shed in beauty, and roses bloom and tender chervil and flowery melilot.[7]

H.D. has given us her own succinct descriptions of these women who formed such a constant and vital matrix of presence in Sappho's work, in "The Wise Sappho:"

> I love to think of Atthis and Andromeda curled on a sun-baked marble bench like the familiar Tanagra group, talking it over. What did they say? What did

they think? Doubtless, they thought little or nothing and said much.

There is another girl, a little girl. Her name is Cleis. It is reported that the mother of Sappho was named Cleis. It is said that Sappho had a daughter whom she called Cleis. . . I see her heaping shells, purple and rose-edged, stained here and there with saffron colours, shells from Adriatic waters heaped in her own little painted bowl and poured out again and gathered up only to be spilt once more across the sands. We have seen Atthis of yester-year; Andromeda of "fair requital," Mnasidika with provoking length of over-shapely limbs; Gyrinno, loved for some appealing gesture or strange resonance of voice or skill of finger-tips, though failing in the essential and more obvious qualities of beauty; Eranna with lips curved contemptuously over slightly irregular though white and perfect teeth; angry Eranna who refused everyone and bound white violets only for the straight hair she herself braided with precision and cruel self-torturing neatness about her own head. We know of Gorgo, over-riotous, too heavy, with special intoxicating sweetness, but exhausting, a girl to weary of, no companion, her over-soft curves presaging early development of heavy womanhood.

Among the living there are these and others. Timas, dead among the living, lying with lily wreath and funeral torch, a golden little bride, lives though sleeping more poignantly even than the famous Graeco-Egyptian beauty the poet's brother married at Naucratis. Rhodope, a name redolent (even though we may no longer read the tribute of the bridegroom's sister) of the heavy out-curling, over-lapping petals of the peerless flower.[8]

Obviously Sappho had a group around her; in fact, she would later be called a whore for having so many women lovers in her life. From all appearances, they constituted a "community" to themselves, for some period of their lives at least. She seems to have kept track of them even when they had left her company, and often it appears they left her company only to go to that of another woman, women known as "Sappho's rivals." This is an interpretation based on a belief that women's relationships consist of either/or competition. In the Lesbian community as it exists in modern times, a "rival" may also be one's best friend, ex-lover, or lover-to-be, and the operation of jealousy is not so simple as it seems. Jealousy and other strong emotions, as well as love and desire, have to do with maintaining a network of Lesbians who support each other long after, or prior to, or in spite of never having been, lovers with each other.

For though Lesbian communities have been reduced since Sappho's time to a public example of two lovers, as in Gertrude and Alice, or one lonely Emily Dickinson pining after her brother's wife, such isolation is only public. The matrix underlying all Lesbian love is extensive and involves a group effort, and some sort of network of support from other women, women who are not Lesbian.

With the decline of the gynarchic states that set the stage for a poet such as Sappho in the first place, the community of women as a public force declined. It cloistered, and it survived in informal networks. It surfaced for several decades in the South of France during the twelfth century in concert with the women troubadors and other Gay and woman-centered social elements. After the women troubadors lived there that area was a center of widespread heresy in the 13th century, heresy that encouraged female as well as Gay leadership, the worship of a two-sided deity, Gay and other libertarian sexual customs. The language of the troubadours is rich with imagery from the female domain, of roses and hearts, chalices, and utter devotion to ideals and to love. But this movement was warred upon and swept under by the heavy hand of the

54

Inquisition. Vestiges of a public women's community went underground with the whores, witches, Lesbians and other fairy people.

In the nineteenth century, Emily Dickinson, isolated spinster *par excellance*, had the presence of other women in her life and their dedication saved her work from extinction. Her friendly editor Thomas Higginson treated her like an exotic pet, did not really like her work and discouraged her from publishing it, although that seems to have been what she wanted more than anything. After her death it was the women related to her who put her poems into print. They managed to do this despite their fear of disclosing the sheer overtness of Emily's Lesbian feelings, which almost caused sister-in-law Sue Dickinson to destroy the packets of hand-written manuscripts. The packets were literally saved by Emily's faithful younger sister Lavinia. In trying to edit the controversial material decades after it was written, Sue's daughter, Martha Dickinson Bianchi, censored the Lesbian references from Dickinson's letters and poems before publishing very bland renditions of the poet's actual sentiments. But in spite of their difficulties with the overtly Lesbian and more sharp-tongued parts, they retained her work and they made it public, even in the absence of a real women's community.

And then, astoundingly, as the twentieth century opened, it all began to re-form: a vocally growing feminism, the open expression and development of a Lesbian community, and a public expression of the centrality of women to themselves. With Amy Lowell and her lover Ada Russell, this expression took the form of a coterie of Lesbian friends who kept in contact with each other, visited each other, influenced each other. They also had tremendous impact on twentieth century ideas and literature. This network of friends included H.D. and the novelist Bryher, who had a covert Lesbian marriage and child-rearing arrangement together, though the image projected by and about H.D. is that she was ambivalent about Lesbianism. She continually idealized male lovers; she was uncertain enough about being taken seriously as the brillant female intelligence that she was that she used as a pen name her initials, H.D., instead of her name Hilda Doolittle. But she spent the greater portion of her adult life — more than forty years — in relation to Bryher; Bryher was her island from which she wrote. The main body of her work is a deep, intense exploration of female powers, couched in metaphoric structures drawn from classical Greek mythology and the Egyptian occult tradition.

Other early twentieth century Lesbian writers who followed on Dickinson's Victorian/Calvinist heels were able to be openly or at least semi-openly Lesbian in the company of other poets, could even form a social group with them. So the very dykish Lowell stayed influential with the Imagiste movement that included Ezra Pound, D.H. Lawrence and William Carlos Williams, as well as H.D.. And the very dykely novelist, Bryher, though she apparently had a terrible reputation among the men as a termagant and other frighteningly "butch" things, was at least moderately acceptable to H.D.'s peer's in the literary society so vital to all of their work.

Gertrude Stein in her beautiful and outrageous Caesar haircut is most well known for her position among prominent male artists of the century, but she and Alice were also part of a network of Lesbian friends. Those dinner parties, of course, did not receive public attention, yet they happened; I dare say they were sustaining.

Networks of contemporary women sustain Lesbian writers; and the writers themselves look to their own heritage for food and drink and direction. Dickinson had certainly read Sappho, though she was most directly and deeply influenced by Elizabeth Barrett Browning. Amy Lowell expressed fierce loyalty to the women poets who had gone before her. Jean Gould, in her biography *Amy: The World of Amy Lowell and the Imagist Movement* wrote this description of Lowell's devotion to her sister writers:

> Her poem, "The Sisters," opening with a meditation on the "family" of women poets, was published in the *North American Review*. This was the poem in which

she stated her views on the "queer lot" they were. . . In "The Sisters" she paid tribute to three poets she much admired. Of "Sapho" she said: "And she is Sapho— Sapho—not Miss or Mrs." But the next poet, "Mrs. Browning," of whom she is very fond, she would never dream of calling "Ba," and says bitterly, ". . . as if I didn't know / What those years felt like tied down to the sofa. / Confounded Victoria, and the slimy inhibitions she loosed on all us Anglo-Saxon creatures!" The third "sister," Emily Dickinson, she could not bring herself to address as "Miss Dickinson," or send a formal visiting card; in her fantasy meeting with Emily, she "climbed over the fence, and found her deep / Engrossed in the doing of a humming-bird / Among nasturtiums." She called Emily a "Frail little elf, / The lonely brain-child of a gaunt maturity," who "hung her womanhood upon a bough / And played ball with the stars—too long— too long long— / Until at last she lost even the desire / To take it down." Amy blamed not only Queen Victoria again, but also Martin Luther, "And behind him the long line of Church Fathers / Who draped their prurience like a dirty cloth / About the naked majesty of God."[9]

The connections of contemporary Lesbian poets to each other, though they may have developed late, are of vital importance to the growth of our ideas. Of the contemporary Lesbian poets under discussion, Adrienne Rich has written about H.D., Dickinson, Lowell, Stein, Lorde and myself. Olga Broumas has credited Sappho and Rich (along with Sylvia Plath, Anne Sexton, Virginia Woolf); Allen has written about my work and Lorde's; with this essay I have now written about, and do hereby credit as influences, all of them, beginning about 1977, except for Lorde, whose work I was beginning to know and utterly love by 1971.[10] I am saying all these names as a way of showing the lineage, and how conscious it has been. We have consciously drawn from a tradition leading back to Sappho and to a House of Women whether we have called it that or not.

Writing from a House of Women Out Into the World

The decision an artist makes, to speak for women and to speak as a woman (and likewise as a member of any group, a Lesbian, a Jewish, Black, working class person, etc.) is probably the most powerful decision she will make. For in making it, she chooses autonomy, she chooses to stand somewhere in particular to speak out to her society. Her work, in locating itself so specifically socially and historically takes on a power it cannot have if she chooses, instead, to speak anonymously, "universally." But having made this choice, she faces another danger, for if she addresses only members of her special groups, her work will have limited power, and limited integrity. It is the acknowledgement and then the inclusion of *all* our selves that leads us to the idea of life as consisting of many expanding, multicultural worlds in which everyone is ultimately included (as well as excluded).

This expansion happens after the artist plants herself in the midst of all her groups, and embraces the cultural separatism that enables autonomy, self-definition and community to develop. From this strong home-base, then, she can approach the world at large as somebody in particular, as Sappho did when she bragged that no one could out-sing the poets of Lesbos.

If the network, or base of women bonded as lovers and as friends is home base for the Lesbian poets, it is not for its own sake only. It has not been for the purpose of aggrandizing Lesbianism, nor even of "making the world a safer place," for Lesbianism (though that is sometimes a necessary effect). Rather it has been a place from which to speak and a lens through which to view our society at large. It is paradoxically both a central and an "outsider" position from which to take a stance.

In finding an appropriate voice with which to speak from her own highly eccentric dykely life, Amy Lowell was drawn to and highly influential within what Ezra Pound named the "Imagist Movement" of poetry. Imagism is poetry in which romantic sludge and conventional metaphor, rhyme schemes and taken-for-granted ideas were stripped away, sheared off to leave a crisp emphasis on the image alone, the image itself to convey meaning. This left the mind's eye free to make new conections, free of nineteenth century values. The Imagists, and Amy Lowell in particular, looked to the literature of American Indians, especially Pueblo Indians, who she openly imitated in a series of poems. She also drew from early Chinese and Japanese forms to find a cleanness of line and thought, a spareness of obvious truth. In her very ambitious and productive way Lowell was so busy an organizer of the Imagist Movement and supporter of the other Imagist writers that Pound later, and in disgust, called it the "Amigist Movement."

Lowell concentrated her artistic energies on stripping the poem to a clean, spare image, on writing in almost terse, "Americanized" poetic sentences, though still keeping to schemes of rhyme and rhythm that were relatively tight (compared to Whitman, who had opened sentences to loquacious freedom forty years earlier). Lowell began using coarse, startling, formerly unacceptable phrases, descriptions and ideas. The Harvard society of her father and brothers found the lines in her poem "Grotesque" to be insulting: "Why do the lillies goggle their tongues at me / . . . / Why do they shriek your name / And spit at me. . . "[11]

Not that she didn't wax beautifully lyrical much of the time, especially in her love poems to Ada. In "Song for a Viola d'Amore," she writes:

> The lady of my choice is bright
> As a clematis at the touch of night,
> As a white clematis with a purple heart
> When twilight cuts the earth and sun apart[12]

"Patterns" is virtually the only poem of Lowell's to have been so heavily anthologized as to keep her name alive today, when her work is out of print and difficult to find. In this poem she translated the social strictures and pressures she felt on her own Lesbian life into a poem about a woman who is buttoned into the whalebone and brocade of rigid social convention. The woman walks in a lush, promising and sensual garden with her male lover, unable to give herself over to her passion though she is able to fantasize a naked embrace with him. As the poem proceeds we see that she is reading a letter announcing that the lover has been killed in battle, and all their careful adherence to sexual strictures has been for nothing. The poem's ending line, "Christ! what are patterns for," combines a bitter curse, a naming of the responsible party, and a crying out to god, all at one time. The words still shock, and in 1915 they were considered extremely coarse language for a poet, let alone an upper class lady poet, to use.

The emotional substance of "Patterns" came from her own life with Ada Russell, and from the social restrictions they felt about being a queer couple. Jean Gould says in her biography that after writing "Patterns" the poet was "so buoyant over achieving exactly the effect she desired that she could hardly wait for Ada's opinion, and she met her at the door with it when her friend came home."[13]

In "Patterns," Amy was writing out from a base of Lesbian love, out from it into the world at large, translating her own experience into terms a wide and heterosexual audience could instantly identify with. In so doing, she spoke against all moral strictures, for all who wanted to break with Victorian morality, for all who understood that the sexual inhibitions had something to do with the "pattern called war."

"Imagism" set up a form of new lyricism that H.D. fully developed after her early "Imagist" years. She turned to an astonishing, breathtaking epic poetry, where she explored epic themes in tight, precise, lyric couplets. The pairing together of the two forms was essential for her task of writing modern mythic-occult-prophetic-historic-epics from *within* a female point of view. With her form she, like Sappho, is able to portray both the inside world and the outside world: both the narrative of what happened and the inner dialogue of what the experience felt, looked, tasted, smelled like.

In her form, she married the female/lyric/Sapphic and the male/epic/narrative/Homeric. She reversed their effects: the usually "objective" narration of events is focused on an internal/occult landscape:

> Clytaemnestra gathered the red rose,
> Helen, the white,
> but they grew on one stem,
>
> one branch, one root in the dark;
> I have not answered his question,
> which was the veil?
>
> which was the dream?
> was the dream, Helen upon the ramparts?
> was the veil, Helen in Egypt?[14]

The usually cold external narrative is told in a warm, lyric, personal voice; yet the story being told is epic, is history:

> Be still, I say, strive not,
> yourself to annul the decree;
> you can not return to the past
>
> nor stay the sun in his course;
> be still, I say, why weep?
> you spoke of your happiness,
>
> I was near you and heard you speak;
> I heard you question Achilles
> and Achilles answer you;
>
> be still, O sister, O shadow;
> your sister, your shadow was near,
> lurking behind the pillars,
>
> counting the fall of your feet,
> as Achilles beneath the ramparts;
> you spoke and I heard you speak;. . . [15]

Perhaps only a woman who loved both women and men in her life could have accomplished, would have attempted, such a wedding of forms, forms that have been considered oppositional.

Turning the Inside Outside: Gertrude Stein

A classic dyke in form and function, Gertrude Stein sat with the male artists and intellectuals who visited the home she and Alice Toklas kept in Paris. She did not sit with the wives of the artists; she was a woman who crossed over into a man's world of writing and innovating literature. "I will come back a lion," she said of her move to Europe, and she meant a literary lion, not a pussy cat. And perhaps Alice did not want her sitting with the wives, and be subject to their flirting. Alice, after all, was the wife of an artist too, an artist named Gertrude, though unlike those other wives, Toklas' name is remembered. Women were the main subject of Stein's art; she wrote of them in portraits and stories, myths and poems, using humor, sensitivity, sensuality, commentary, description. She wrote *as* a woman of her times, using an interior female landscape. Mundane female objects and scenes were her field of study: furniture, pictures, cows, poodles, people at dinner, people in love, people talking together. For Stein, the House of Women was her own house, and her own female perspective on the nature of the house, as she developed it in the close companionship she shared with Toklas.

Writing out from the base of a woman to woman relationship considered taboo in the world, and translating this everyday personal experience into a literature that no longer overtly contains the taboo experience yet covertly contains it in great detail was a lifelong preoccupation of Gertrude Stein. In gaining the ability to put into her work the love between herself and Alice Toklas, she not only stripped poetry to the spare image, she also stripped away image and entered the domain of language itself. Once into that world, she began perceiving and treating words as individual bricks that have a free-floating meaning of their own, unattached to the automatic cliched meanings they have in sentence form.

By detaching verbs from nouns, by detaching linear plot from language, taking apart the old formula that noun acts upon object and verb is amplified by adverb, she opened up the nature of language itself, made spaces in it. Into these spaces of "free floating" or uncliched meaning, she dropped the substance and the everyday happenings of her life with Alice, including their erotic life, their pet names for each other and their highly personal ways of being together. She did this with such subtlety that only one poem was considered overtly homosexual enough to be included in the *Penguin Book of Homosexual Verse*:

> I love my love with a v
> Because it is like that
> I love my love with a b
> Because I am beside that
> A king.
> I love my love with an a
> Because she is a queen
> I love my love and a a is the best of them
> Think well and be a king,
> Think more and think again
> I love my love with a dress and a hat
> I love my love and not with this or with that
> I love my love with a y because she is my bride
> I love her with a d because she is my love beside
> Thank you for being there
> Nobody has to care
> Thank you for being here
> Because you are not there.
> And with and without me which is and without she
> can be late   she
> and then and how and all around we think and found that
>   it

63

is time to cry
she and I.[16]

Stein opened up language itself, the very bricks of it, the very
of of it, the it of it, the the of of. Amy Lowell and the Imagists had
stripped poetry free of the sultry, stultifying imagery of the Victorian age in order to allow for a more "modern" content — and in
Lowell's case at least, a more Lesbian content. Gertrude Stein
stripped the structure of the language itself. She collapsed into one
voice the two supposedly oppositional extremes of perception —
objective and subjective — collapsed them into one form, one
technique, one mode of understanding. The result is a truer form
of objectivity, a virtually value-free language, as well as a truer
form of subjectivity, an almost ego-free and sentiment-free experience of the work.

By equalizing the value of each word, Stein was locating the
commonness of language, the equality of value each word has with
every other. She treated each word as a unit of meaning in and of
itself, taking the meaning new each time from the context of the
other words around it, and also from the multitude of associations
we make in our inner brains, in our word-poetic minds of simple association.

In exploring this terrain she freed language from its linear
plot. Not only did she free the image from the old romantic affilia-
tions as Lowell and the Imagists did, but she also freed each sentence from its linear plot of grammar: subject is a noun acting with
a verb upon a subject and is modified by adjectives. She made
nouns out of articles and verbs out of nouns and subjects out of
adverbs and conjunctions. And in so doing she took all the moral
judgmentalness from language, all the expectation: hero saves
heroine from evil landlord. She removed all the expectation: this
is good, this is bad, this is indifferent. In her sentences each word
is indifferent, is good and is bad. Each word is evil, is a landlord,
a heroine, is saving. And so she was able to use the substance of her
inner life, her home life, her personal life and those of *all* her
friends, not merely the socially acceptable ones. And because she

had freed the language of all possible judgment there is no way to read her work and to judge her life in any terms except her own. It takes a very wild and major lion to do this, to set the terms of value, to the art.

Consider this passage from "Lifting Belly":

Lifting belly with me.
You inquire.
What you do then.
Pushing.
Thank you so much.
And lend a hand.
What is lifting belly now.
My baby.
Always sincerely.
Lifting belly says it there.
Thank you for the cream.
Lifting belly tenderly.
A remarkable piece of intuition.
I have forgotten all about it.
Have you forgotten all about it.
Little nature which is mine.
Fairy ham
Is a clam.
Of chowder
Kiss him Louder.
Can you be especially proud of me.
Lifting belly a queen.
In that way I can think.
Thank you so much.
I have,
lifting belly for me.
I can not forget the name.
lifting belly for me.
Lifting belly again.

Can you be proud of me.
I am.
Then we say it.
In miracles.
Can we say it and then sing. You mean drive.
I mean drive.
We are full of pride.
Lifting belly is proud.
Lifting belly is my queen.
Lifting belly happy.
Lifting belly see.
lifting belly.
Lifting belly address.
Little washers.
Lifting belly how do you do.
Lifting belly is famous for recipes.
You mean Genevieve.
I mean I never ask for potatoes.
But you liked them then.
And now.
Now we know about water.
Lifting belly is a miracle.
And the Caesars.
The Caesars are docile.
Not more docile than is right.
No beautifully right.
And in relation to a cow.
And in relation to a cow.
Do believe me when I incline.
You mean obey.
I mean obey.
Obey me.
Husband obey your wife.
Lifting belly is so dear.
To me.

Lifting belly is smooth,
Tell lifting belly about matches.
Matches can be struck with the thumb.
Not by us.
No indeed.
What is it I say about letters.
Twenty six.
And counted.
And counted deliberately.
This is not as difficult as it seems.
Lifting belly is so strange.
And quick.
Lifting belly in a minute.
Lifting belly in a minute now.
In a minute.
Not to-day.
No not to-day.
Can you swim.
Lifting belly can perform aquatics.
Lifting belly is astonishing.
Lifting belly for me.
Come together.
Lifting belly near.
I credit you with repetition.
Believe me I will not say it.
And retirement.
I celebrate something.
Do you.[17]

Looking at the outside from the inside and at the inside from
the outside, Stein fulfilled her function of Lesbian poet to the
highest degree. She also achieved a singular objectivity with this
method, especially about highly charged social stigmas. After
shelving as unpublishable her first, and completely Lesbian, novel
of a triangle of young women, she proceeded to write *Three Lives*,
three portraits of women very different from herself and from each

other. The first of these, "Melanctha" is virtually the only example in literature of a white author writing of Black characters simply for themselves, and, like the Lesbians in her first novel, portrayed solely in relation to each other rather than to the outside (and white) world. Language conventions for describing race change so rapidly from decade to decade, that "Melanctha" may appear inappropriate to us in ways that were certainly not true when it was written.

From her early and relatively concrete, linear works ("Melanctha" has a recognizable plot, for instance) she continued to experiment more and more with the nature of language, thought and communication itself. In *The Making of Americans* (of which it is joked that only Toklas, who typed it, has read the whole thing), and in her erotic poems such as "Lifting Belly," and even more in her later plays, she treated language as a real being, plastic rather than fixed. Her language creates context rather than being contextual. She was exploring the neurological impressions and connections words make inside our brains. Modern psychologists, also being, as Stein was earlier, students of the great psychologist William James, would do this themselves in developing behaviorism and neurolinguistics.

Concerning naming she said, very specifically:

So then in Tender Buttons I was making poetry but and it seriously troubled me, dimly I knew that nouns made poetry but in prose I no longer needed the help of nouns and in poetry did I need the help of nouns. Was there not a way of naming things that would not invent names, but mean names without naming them.

I had always been very impressed from the time that I was very young by having had it told me and then afterwards feeling it myself that Shakespeare in the forest of Arden had created a forest without mentioning the things that make a forest. You feel it all but he does not name its names. . .

I commenced trying to do something in Tender Buttons about this thing. I went on and on trying to do this thing. I remember in writing An Acquaintance With Description looking at anything until something that was not the name of that thing but was in a way that actual thing would come to be written.

Naturally, and one may say that is what made Walt Whitman naturally that made the change in the form of poetry, that we who had known the names so long did not get a thrill from just knowing them. We that is any human being living has inevitably to feel the thing anything being existing, but the name of that thing of that anything is no longer anything to thrill anyone except children. So as everybody has to be a poet, what was there to do. This that I have just described, the creating it without naming it, was what broke the rigid form of the noun the simple noun poetry which now was broken.[18]

In collapsing the external and the internal into one view, lining them up on one single plane of being she is using a technique similar to that used by tribal poetry, by American Indian poetry, for example. She reversed the belief that so much Western writing and Western science has had: that one must and can choose between the internal and the external vision, can split them. (They are usually split artificially along gender line, racial lines, and class lines.) But if we deny the internal we cannot see the external very clearly either, and vice versa, although we can have the emotional illusion of clear perception. This is a culture-trance, a mythic story all participants give as "reasons" for their feelings and behavior in any given situation.[19]

By unifying the internal and external viewpoints, and by assigning equal value to each component of her work, each letter of the word, each word of the sentence, each image being described, Stein enabled a nonlinear, democratic and powerfully female landscape of the mind; she literally dis-enchanted the mythic "sleep," the "culture trance" or previous myths of Western partriarchal literature, and she did this primarily through her approach to language.

Toward a Contemporary Lesbian House of Women

For contemporary Lesbian poets who have undertaken a definition of the word "Lesbian" and its many implications, and who deliberately have established as large as possible a "house" of women based on bonding in the most essential ways, three major areas have concerned us. These are self-determination, autonomy and community, the same concerns that preoccupy any group attempting to maintain its identity in a hostile environment.

All these qualities seem implicitly present in Sappho's work. Certainly she had a community of women around her, even whose names are known to us; she had vital importance to her culture, as her popularity attests; she had an intact ceremony, a mythos, from which to draw connection to the forces of the universe. Her definitions, like her gods, were her own.

"As for him who finds fault with us, may silliness and sorrow overtake him,"[20] goes one popular poster version of one of her fragments, but nothing indicates it was the female-bonded culture she represented that anyone in her day would find fault with. Her words and definitions were hers, for her teaching, praying, singing purposes, delivered outward to the world from her position of female centrality in her society. An ancient writer named Demetrius said of her, "This is why when Sappho sings of beauty her words are beautiful and sweet; so too when she sings of loves and spring and the halcyon: every type of beautiful word is woven into her poetry, and some of them are her own creation."[21]

The effort of establishing and re-confirming self-definition in the voices of the contemporary Lesbian poets, has included reclaiming words with loaded, stereotypic content such as, Lesbian, dyke, whore, cunt, mother, daughter, birthing and the like — and extending as a matter of the course of our lives into the other groups to which we also variously belong: Black, feminist, working class, Jewish, fat, Indian, alcoholic, intellectual, literary, leftist, mystic, revolutionary, and immigrant American. The effort of reconstructing a female self-definition also has included filling in the silences first pointed out by working class and feminist writer Tillie Olsen, and taken up by Adrienne Rich in her essays and her book *On Lies, Secrets and Silence.*

The leadership exerted by Lesbian and feminist poets as the mass movements of women developed during the 1970's cannot be exaggerated. Even well into the 80's I can hardly walk into a women's center anywhere in the country without seeing lines from any of a dozen of my own poems posted on the wall as mottoes of strength and inspiration to all who pass through. We have all been recorded, reproduced in all manner of media and read by millions of women (and men). Audre Lorde's poetic political stances have become ethical guidelines in more than one sector and so have Adrienne Rich's.

Poets — both feminist and Lesbian — but especially Lesbian/feminist, have repeatedly surfaced with the key words and phrases that later became full-blown movement issues and obsessions. These have included many aspects of sexism and the belittling of women, details of homophobia and compulsory heterosexuality, rape, alcoholism and its debilitating effects on our lives, and racism between women, to use some more obvious examples. Sometimes the poets write out of group consciousness as it develops among active people around them; sometimes they speak from their own individual courage and integrity. Sometimes they have absorbed the ensuing attacks of doubt and hostility as the issue is argued into a public life of its own. Always they are operating as Sappho operated, as any true poet operates: defining the culture around her, giving it name, substance and rhythm so it can grow into a full life.

The development of genuine autonomy has been a second great work undertaken by modern Lesbian feminists and given much attention by the poets. This has included stressing the necessity for women to begin, and to continue, looking to each other and to ourselves for our value and sense of esteem, looking to sameness and commonality for strength and motivation. Pat Parker in the last stanza of a poem called "GROUP" names a major source of reclaimed self-love after it has been torn from us, in this case by racism as well as sexism and homophobia. After describing lessons she learned of hatred of herself for looking Black, and from being called bad, "I do have memory of teachers / you are heathens / why can't you be / like the white kids / you are bad —" she concluded:

> now
> there are new lessons
> new teachers
> each week I go to my group
> see women
> Black women
> Beautiful Black Women
> & I am in love
> with each of them
> & this is important
> in the loving
> in the act of loving
> each woman
> I have learned a new lesson
> I have learned
> to love myself[22]

The Rise of The Common Woman

With the appearance of *The Common Woman Poems*, which I published in 1969 in a basement mimeograph machine edition, the Lesbian and all manner of other "exotic" female experiences were placed — literally speaking — in a framework of commonality and at the *center* of female experience. "The common woman is a common as good bread, and will rise," the poems ended and they were quoted and sloganized over a million times in media that ranged from television to T-shirts.

Adrienne Rich commented on them: "The 'Common Woman' is far more than a class description. What is 'common' in and to women is the intersection of oppression and strength, damage and beauty. It is, quite simply, the *ordinary* in women which will 'rise' in every sense of the word — spiritually and in activism. For us, to be 'extraordinary' or 'uncommon' is to fail. History has been embellished with 'extraordinary,' and 'exemplary,' 'uncommon,' and of course 'token' women whose lives have left the rest unchanged. The 'common woman' is in fact the embodiment of the extraordinary will-to-survive in millions of women, a life-force which transcends childbearing: unquenchable, chromosomatic reality. Only when we can count on this force in each other, everywhere, know absolutely that it is there for us, will we cease abandoning and being abandoned by 'all of our lovers.' "[23]

By placing one Lesbian portrait into a matrix of seven portraits of seven women, I was writing out of the Lesbian couple bond (influenced by the feminist movement) into a much larger world of women in general, who can be seen as and can act as a group based on their commonality, their common interest in improving their lives, and their common strengths of experience and heritage. The idea of common women passed on into Adrienne Rich's *The Dream of A Common Language* where it was greatly broadened by new phrases. The "Common Dream" was a common dream of women together, of the social implications and possibilities of the bond of women, to each other and to their own strengths and powers. This, she suggested, could be articulated by a common language, a "whole new poetry," called for in "Transcendental Etude."[24] By 1976, Olga Broumas would be confident enough about the possibility of a female language to write:

A woman-made
language would
have as many synonyms for pink

light-filled
holy as
the Eskimo does
for snow. [25]

Lesbian and feminist groups of all descriptions have used the word "common" in one capacity or another, to name stores, restaurants, health collectives, or newsletters and magazines, as Midwest Lesbians did with "Common Lives/Lesbian Lives." Lesbian poets have repeated the idea frequently: Broumas mentions "common protest" in her poem "Snow White," and entering "into the common, suspended disbelief of love."[26] Alice Bloch calls her life with her lover our "common life" in a bitter poem expressing lack of social acknowledgement and support for Lesbian relationships.[27]

One critic has pointed out the all-important difference between "universal" and "common" as it has been explored in my work and in Adrienne Rich's. "Common refers to that which is shared; that which no matter how incomplete, as life is incomplete, no matter how imperfect — essentially non-ideal — exists here, now, in its particularity as true." And again, "We do not lose ourselves to find ourselves, we *find* ourselves to find ourselves."[28] Universal, "one-world" implies everyone having to fit into one standard (and of course that one, that "uni," is going to turn out to be a white, male, heterosexual, young, educated, middle class, etc. model). For if there can only be one model, how can it be otherwise? *This* is the white man's burden, to have to be the center for everyone. Common means many-centered, many overlapping islands of groups each of which maintains its own center and each of which is central to society for what it gives to society.

Critic Mary Carruthers has called my "She Who" poems a virtual book of common prayer for women,[29] and that was what I intended when I wrote the bulk of them over a nine month period in 1972. At that time the vision of commonality was solidifying into something both larger and smaller, but certainly more concrete. We were busy establishing a base of female controlled institutions that would begin to answer to the expressed needs of all kinds of women. Women were dramatically shifting the focus of their lives, entering the work force, changing their family structures, bonding with different kinds of lovers than they had ever imagined for themselves, launching careers and starting businesses. Commonality gave way to community, the attempt to concretize the bonding of women into a group identity.

Not surprisingly, the "She Who" poems were written while I was living in a household consisting entirely of Lesbians — some forty of them living there during a five year period. The "She Who" series ends with a list of "every kind of woman I could think of" — and the imagery is not limited to the United States nor to women in the industrial state.

> . . .
> the woman who escaped from the jailhouse
> the woman who is walking across the desert
> the woman who buries the dead
> the woman who taught herself writing
> the woman who skins rabbits
> the woman who believes her own word
> the woman who chews bearskin
> the woman who eats cocaine
> the woman who thinks about everything
> the woman who has the tattoo of a bird
> the woman who puts things together
> the woman who squats on her haunches
> the woman whose children are all different   colors
>
> singing   I am the will of the woman
>   the woman
>   my will is unbending
>
> when She-Who-moves-the-earth will turn over
> when She Who moves, the earth will turn over[30]

In each case, I had a specific person in mind, someone I knew or had read about. For instance, "the woman whose children are all different colors" was in honor of Diane DiPrima, who I have always admired for her free-wheeling choice of fathers for her five children.

The kind of international connection present in the "She Who" series is vividly apparent in Audre Lorde's work. In the startling, physically charged love poem, "Meet," the lovers are not only united with women in all parts of history, including the old slave trading ports of Palmyra and Abomey-Calavi, but also with the earth's own substance and the animal world, especially the lion family:

> Woman when we met on the solstice
> high over halfway between your world and mine
> rimmed with full moon and no more excuses
> your red hair burned my fingers as I spread you
> tasting your ruff down to sweetness
> and I forgot to tell you
> I have heard you calling across this land
> in my blood before meeting
> and I greet you again
> on the beaches in mines lying on platforms
> in trees full of tail-tail birds flicking
> and deep in your caverns of decomposed granite
> even over my own laterite hills
> after a long journey
> licking your sons
> while you wrinkle your nose at the stench.
>
> Coming to rest
> in the open mirrors of your demanded body
> I will be black light as you lie against me
> I will be heavy as August over your hair
> our rivers flow from the same sea
> and I promise to leave you again
> full of amazement and our illuminations
> dealt through the short tongues of color
> or the taste of each other's skin as it hung
> from our childhood mouths. . .

Taste my milk in the ditches of Chile and Ouagadougou
in Tema's bright port while the priestess of Larteh
protects us
in the high meat stalls of Palmyra and Abomey-Calavi
now you are my child and my mother
we have always been sisters in pain.

Come in the curve of the lion's bulging stomach
lie for a season out of the judging rain
we have mated we have cubbed
we have high time for work and another meeting
women exchanging blood
in the innermost rooms of moment
we must taste of each other's fruit
at least once
before we shall both be slain.[31]

Commonality means we get to belong to a number of overlapping groups, not just one. Audre Lorde's work speaks out of the
experiences and urgent concerns of the Black community which
she uses as a base from which to speak to the white community
most critically of murderous, neglectful and defensive white racist
behavior. From the base of Lesbian/feminism she has been able to
speak critically of Black attitudes painful to her; and now from her
newest base of Black and Third World women, including Lesbians, she is speaking critically of the treatment of Black women
by Black men in poems such as "Need: A Choral for Black
Women's Voices."[32] By standing in so many places, she is able to
teach a philosophy of wholeness, of all our splintered selves that
need to be brought together in love, in anger, in pain, in refusal to
lie, in listening, in desire, in greatness of thought, in common
understandings.

The movement of the modern Lesbian poet has been toward
establishing a Woman's House of Power and Unity from which to
speak as a healing and critiquing voice, directly into each community of which we are a part — and these are specific to each author
and diverse from each other.

So we find Paula Gunn Allen working to create a body of literary criticism that will, first, define and clarify the emerging literature of American Indians as a whole, and more recently, concentrating on the women writers of that group. We find Adrienne Rich writing of her life in a half-Jewish family in the Lesbian anthology *Nice Jewish Girls*. Her latest poem, "Sources," ends with a declaration that she will claim her Jewish heritage and it will be from the perspective of women and the power of women. And my most recent poems, *The Queen of Wands*, are more related to my mother's life and the tradition of the heterosexual European folk-goddess Helen, than to my own personal life as a Lesbian. (Yet Helen is a large part of me, too.)

Common Likeness, Common Difference

A most interesting development of the idea of commonality has appeared in the term "common differences:" defining and retaining racial and ethnic identities without losing either our affinity as women and or as Lesbians. This means acknowledging that more than one island of centrality exists, more than one "House of Women" is operating. We can see this while still keeping the continual underlying capacity to learn from, listen to and love, protect and support each other. This involves listening with an open heart to *how* we differ, even inside a common structure. Knowing also, as Lorde has pointed out repeatedly, "other" is an aspect of ourselves projected.

"The Garden" from *Shadow Country* by Paula Gunn Allen is one of a number of poems that speaks directly into the idea of common differences:

scene i

sky still bright
we weed, companionable.
she on her side of the low wall
me on mine

"they leave their shells in the ground"
she says, "see these holes? I don't know
why, they have to be dug up and
thrown away." she holds up
a transparent thing,
tissue pattern for an insect dress.
her petunias, my corn, beans, squash and I
nod amiably.

in the hills last night
two more animals
dismembered:
rectum, lip, nostril, vagina
split.
bodies left bloodless
on the unmarked grass.
something out there.
something unknown.
I straighten, groaning
wipe sweat from my eyes.
mystic impulse all around
slicing holes in air
digging bad dreams
in daylight.
sun like a corpse over me.
sky blooming deep.
a shroud.

    scene ii

unmannered.
soft as night.
air keening.
sky building.
what manners these?
fear lightly easing itself over
back wall, through trees.

starshine
beginning at the edge.
her dress moves with ease, eyes
glitter, hair
so soft in evening wind, she
recalls summer nights,
arms like branches singing, body
sinking graceful into dusk.
comfort of lounge chair
holds buttocks, back, pliant neck.
she dreams of Pentecost, tongues
of flame above her shining hair,
longs for beatitude, so suited
to this place.
a manner of speaking touches her lips
lightly, careful for her carelessness,
words slip cautiously toward formation,
birds settle in for the night, crying.

daylight evaporates as she swirls
her drink, sips cold with perfect ease
against her teeth, rests against cushions
soft as dissolving clouds
overhead.
trees by the back wall
begin to stir
ominous.
sky goes dark.
she doesn't see,
she doesn't make a sound.
Pentecost shimmers
flows from her hair
between her thighs.

scene iii

light angling
volunteer's face ashen
up two days and nights
starshine is not what
got in her eyes.
he used a knife
on her vagina she tells me,
and maybe the hatchet we found
beside the bed
the blood, my god, she tells me.
outside surgery we stand
uneasy, graceless, longing
for the carelessness of birds.

scene iv

haunted
tissue paper hulls
bad dreams in daylight
no sleep in dark
before my eye
a shadow
photograph of Brazilian Indian woman hung
by the ankles from a pole
long hair sweeping down
blowing in the laden breeze
white hunter standing next to her
spread legs. she is naked.
she is dead.[33]

"The Garden" is a particularly sharply drawn theme that is a familiar and unresolved one: the two women are placed in a garden, which is their commonality as females, with female traditions. But the reality of what is happening there is entirely different for one than it is for the other. For the shadow woman there is ever-present horror, which she can never lose sight of, for she is never safe and never has the illusion of safety. For the comfortable woman there is obliviousness of danger, of the real nature of her neighbors, of even the nature of the insects in her little garden or the attacks on animals in the hills behind her house. She has the frivolity that results from ignorance and over-shelter. She does not have any idea what the Indian woman sees; and in this poem she makes no attempt to find out. So she is shut out from knowing the other's view of life, but she is also cut off from her own life as well, for one cannot live on petunias and dreams of beatitude. Yet in spite of the denial of the oblivious woman and her inability to acknowledge the danger, let alone protect, they are nevertheless *in fact* united in horror, in blood and in rape.

> Here is what I know:
> Even the most golden
> golden apple sometimes
> rolls down the long wand limb
> and lands in the lap of fire[34]

As Helen says in *The Queen of Wands*.

The fragmentation of the fabric of our myth, the myth connecting us all in a House of Women, a House of Muses, causes pain, anger and the adoption, among Lesbians, of the role of the outcast. Audre Lorde has called her book of political essays *Sister Outsider*; Olga Broumas clearly defines her place among women as "kissing against the light." And in all of our work it is clear we understand our role as that of the outsider. Sappho expressed the feeling: *Like the hyacinth which shepherds tread underfoot in the mountains, and on the ground the purple flower. . .* [35]

Yet "outsider" is only half the term for what we do and know about what we do. For in seeking wholeness, integrity and the utter transformation of our society, we have also been busy reconnecting to the various houses from which we come. As "outsiders" to one culture, we increasingly become insiders to several others. In becoming outsiders to male-defined society we have certainly become insiders to female-defined society.

The Ideal Place of Wholeness Appears in All Our Work

An ideal place appears in much of the imagery of Lesbian poets: in a similar way that Rich has used Stonehenge, H.D. used the white island and the sacred orchard; Lowell used the garden and Dickinson used her own unique concept of "heaven" — not the patriarchal heaven, but the one where she would find her own name and could reunite with her lost female love. In a similar way, Lesbians think of Lesbos as an ideal place, home, where one is central to one's own life, and where the women are bonding, are sisters — and more than sisters. Where there is a House of Women, a myth, a place of centrality.

In each poet this ideal place of wholeness is expressed differently.[36] This place of home base is alternately longed for and defined by Lorde. It is a name she seeks to learn, a "tree under which she is lying," the lover's (that is, Woman's) body she would like to plant crops of the future on.[37]

In Allen's poetry this place is called "home" and home is idea — "an idea of ourselves is what we own."[38] In my work the place itself is found in each other, gained through "work" — by which I mean the yeast of creative effort, as "to work magic" — as well as decision, resolve. With Adrienne Rich, the home place is mind, and choice. From "Twenty-One Love Poems:"

XV

If I lay on that beach with you
white, empty, pure green water warmed by the Gulf
                         Stream
and lying on that beach we could not stay
because the wind drove fine sand against us
as if it were against us
if we tried to withstand it and we failed—
if we drove to another place
to sleep in each other's arms
and the beds were narrow like prisoners' cots

and we were tired and did not sleep together
and this was what we found, so this is what we did—
was the failure ours?
If I cling to circumstances I could feel
not responsible. Only she who says
she did not choose, is the loser in the end.[39]

In "Twenty-One Love Poems," Rich locates a new place, a not-Stonehenge-simply, but the mind "casting back" to a shared solitude "chosen without loneliness." This place equals an end to the alienation that has been the price of forming any little piece of a House of Women bonded — when it has been secretive, as "two against the world." Rich walks into this new place, a place of both "heavy shadows and great light." "I choose to be a figure in that light," she says, "I choose to walk here. And to draw this circle."[40]

Building communities that can center in a House of Women has figured strongly in our work and in our lives also, since we believe our work, and act on it. Building communities means making cross connections and healing the torn places in the social fabric of myth we have all inherited, but that the outcast especially inherits. No trace of this ripped fabric of fragmented life is evident in Sappho's work, besides that the work is itself in fragments, and she herself has been shredded so often. But anti-Lesbianism and institutionalized misogyny developed centuries after she wrote as a highly esteemed citizen in what must have been a remarkably intact holistic society.

Paula Gunn Allen writes of the creatrix, the primary god (Spider Grandmother) of the Keres, an American Pueblo Indian culture:

> . . . she was given the work of weaving the strands
> of her body, her pain, her vision,
> into creation, and the gift of having created,
> to disappear.
> . . . After her I sit on my laddered rain-bearing rug
> and mend the tear with string.[41]

After Sappho the others of us who are doing this work sit mending tears in the fabrics of our myth also, mending the tears in the tales Sappho said Love weaves, mending the tapestries the old women storytellers once made of the substance of a wholistic life, its spider meanings.

We are mending the rips and tears, yes. And we are doing more, we are attempting, I believe, what Stein accomplished when she broke the culture trance between the objective and subjective worlds. We are, each in her own unique way, attempting to completely rearrange a particular way of thinking, to turn it inside out. We are taking on the forces within us and outside us, as Rich says:

> . . .
> this we were, and this is how we tried to love,
> and these are the forces they had ranged against us,
> and these are the forces we had ranged within us,
> within us and against us, against us and within us.[42]

Rich writes into a female version of history and into a sense of the intellect that includes mystic elements to make her demanding critiques of modern civilization. She holds female qualities up as a model for behavior: let the men have the courage of women, she says, and meanwhile in her lover's small, strong hands she can trust the world.

For each of us, the points of contact differ, the Houses of Women have different origins and are woven of slightly different stuff. Broumas, for instance, waded into the common Western European myths of women. Simply by completely restructuring Leda and the Swan, eliminating the former rapist/Zeus/father she rearranged the relation of the female to what impregnates us. The Swan, she said, was another woman. In this outrageous act, she opened the world of Western mythology, so it became easy, even less radical, for me to walk into the myth of Helen in *The Queen of Wands* and interpret it according to my own intuitions, history and research.

I think that it is my ability to place the exotic, extreme and overlooked stereotypes of the female — not only of common women, but of queens and whores, wives and dykes — into a place of tradition and centrality, that gives my work its "re-membering" qualities. It restructures the usual patriarchal myth of female/male class structure. In my work the most hidden, taboo qualities of female life are pulled to the surface and seen not only as charged and magical, but as having integrated mythical reality — as reaching back and forth in time — as defining qualities central to all female-centered power.

Audre Lorde in the special mediumship of her work takes full force the racial as well as sexual stereotyping for the stuff of her exploration of the inside and the outside. The feared "other," she says in dozens of ways, is a projection of ourselves: "I think you / afraid I was mama as laser / seeking to eat out or change your substance" she wrote in "Letter for Jan."[43] She speaks of "all her faces." And in "Dream/Songs From the Moon in Beulah Land," she specifies the special deafness of stereotyping: "If I were drum / you would beat me / listening for the echo / of your own touch."[44] And the functions of the female warrior in our society she defines succinctly and brilliantly:

> I come like a woman
> who I am
> spreading out through nights
> laughter and promise
> and dark heat
> warming whatever I touch
> that is living
> consuming
> only
> what is already dead.[45]

Paula Gunn Allen's work also seeks to unhook a culture trance that has racial definitions as a major basis for its terrible operations. This racial designation, "Indian," is also a metaphor for the whole half-buried tribal world, a world that held spiritual and intellectual understandings far different from those given to us since the downfall of the world of Sappho. In many of her poems, Allen places the material world and the spiritual world in a juxtaposition of idea, tugging and tugging at the Western definitions of what is alive, what is dead, what has meaning.

All of this is conscious effort to alter and break the "culture trance" of the belief system around us, so we can speak our own truths, from the basis of our own lives. We speak them out into a world at large, which then learns its own interpretations and makes its own uses of what we say.

Mythic Realism and a House of Women

Mythic realism is a phrase I have used for years to help myself understand what I am doing and what my contemporaries are doing in their art. I invented it (so far as I know); I was comparing my novel, *The Motherlords* with the artwork of Lesbian artists Wendy Cadden and Karen Sjöholm, and also the artwork of a Black woman who is not a Lesbian, Irmajean. All of them use female subjects portrayed realistically on one level, yet with deep connections to a communally held myth at the same time. Mythic realism means to me that when myth and reality are combined the result is art based on our collective consciousness and collective unconsciousness. Gay writer Robert Gluck, heavily influenced by Lesbian/feminism as well as his own Jewish and Gay cultures, speaks of taking into account both the local (the community and the individual) and the sublime (the unknown and unknowable). The village and the wilderness, as Paula Gunn Allen might say.

Mythic realism describes much of the work of all five contemporary Lesbian poets discussed here. Audre Lorde called *Zami* a "biomythography" from the same perspective.[46] *Zami* is partly a biography, based in physical fact, and partly it is mythic, drawing strong erotic/power essence from the great stream (the cultural dream stream) of Africa/Caribbean/American Black Orisha (gods). In *Zami* this myth is carried in the person of the ever intriguing lover character Kitty, who is really the old female poet-warrior-god Afrikete manifested in the flesh in the Gay culture of Harlem.

We do not take the sacred, the political, the social, the details of everyday, and carry them "away" or split them from each other. We place them all together in the real lives of real women in the present, in the raucous, dangerous, tumultuous marketplace/urban/warzone/suburb of modern life. As Sappho did. In this way we help to re-found a House of Women from which to approach all other worlds, a re-connection to the Roses of the Muses, the intact fabric of the female myth.

Part III

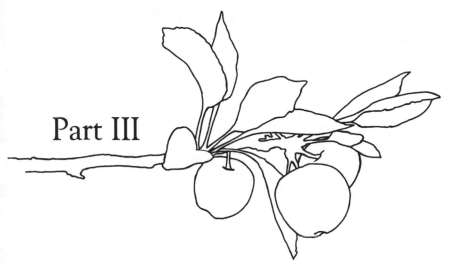

To Surface With Lesbian Gods

To Surface With Lesbian Gods

And Sappho said this: *Hesperus, (evening star) bringing everything that shining Dawn scattered, you bring the sheep, you bring the goat, you bring back the child to its mother.*[1]

Many gods lived in Sappho's world, and her fragments have considerable reference to them. Although her favorite was Aphrodite, also called Cyprus, the Cyprian, after her island of origin, Sappho also speaks of Hermes the cup bearer, of Adonis, Hymen, Hera, Zeus, Ares, Hephaistos, the "holy, rosy-armed" Graces and the Muses.

In some poems she is calling the gods to her: *Hither again, Muses, leaving the golden (house of your father, Zeus)*[2] and *Hither now, tender Graces and lovely-haired Muses.*[3] Quite directly and simply, "come here." In others, she is describing their behavior: *There a bowl of ambrosia had been mixed, and Hermes took the jug and poured wine for the gods.*[4] Or praising their being, as in *Let your (graceful form appear) near me (while I pray), lady Hera. . .*[5]

Beauty, love, grace filled her descriptions of the gods, even in their persons: *It is not easy for us to rival the goddesses in loveliness of figure,*[6] she sang. And in another song, *but I love delicacy. . .love has obtained for me the brightness and beauty of the sun.*[7] Not physical appearance of love and beauty alone does she praise, however, for appropriate behavior also plays a part in her aesthetic teachings: *for he that is beautiful is beautiful as far as appearances go, while he that is good will consequently also be beautiful.*[8]

Many of her fragments appear to be instruction in appropriate behavior and attitudes to bear toward the gods. When she says it is not right that there should be lamentation in the house of those who serve the Muses, the reason given is, *That would not be fitting for us.*[9] In another poem, the speaker asks Aphrodite (here called Cytherea) what to do now that Adonis is dying: *Delicate Adonis is dying, Cytherea; what are we to do?* and the goddess answers with explicit instructions: *Beat your breasts, girls, and tear your clothes.*[10]

The appropriate behavior centered often (or at least the fragments indicate this) on the proper dress for pleasing the gods:

> . . . *and you, Dica, put lovely garlands around your locks,*
> *binding together stems of anise with your soft hands; for the*
> *blessed Graces look rather on what is adorned with flowers*
> *and turn away from the ungarlanded.*[11]

It is monumentally purposeful, then, this wearing of flowers that appears so often in her words; flowers will draw the attention of the gods and spirits, and they will favor us. They are gods who love brightness and heavy odors and vivid colors; they are not gods of severity and deprivation.

In speculating on what the gods, what holiness and spirituality, meant to Sappho (and therefore could possibly mean to us, in our world, and in our traditional connection to her), I have found it useful to look at the names of flowers and colors she mentioned. In poetry that lasts, virtually nothing is accidental or without a larger-than-surface meaning. Flowers have mythic dimension because of the sacred (and otherwise) stories told of them over the centuries.

Lilies, for instance, have become Christian symbols of purity, death and resurrection. The daisy is a homey, trustworthy flower in song and poem representing the loyal love of a good-hearted woman. Neither of these occurs in Sappho's fragments. Her flowers are the rose, violet, hyacinth, golden chick-pea, anise and chervil. The rose, of course, recurs throughout Western literature as the supreme natural manifestation of the essentially female. The red rose signifies power, eroticism and creativity on the deepest levels. Along with the apple, or similar red fruit such as pomegranate, the rose conjures the vulva with its birthing, sexual/creative and menstrual/intuitive powers.

Perhaps, in fact, when Sappho speaks of the reddening sweet-apple at the topmost bough, the one that the apple pickers could not reach — she is singing a womanly song of special protection for the essential female powers: they will never, quite, be reached, and taken from us.

Gold is a color often repeated in Sappho's lines, especially with relation to Aphrodite, god of love, who is described as golden-throned, as golden-crowned, as coming from a golden house, as pouring nectar into golden cups. This seems appropriate for the poet of love, since gold is the traditional color associated with love, as modern wedding ring customs testify. I personally believe that gold is a color seen in a love-induced psychic state. Sappho reported seeing a color that was *more golden than gold*; Aphrodite's head (aura?) she saw as *golden-crowned*, and love was gold-colored to her for she said that *love has obtained for me the brightness and beauty of the sun*.[12]

A color almost as prominent as gold in Sappho's work is purple. In the sparse fragments left of her work there are fourteen references to purple or to violets and other purple flowers. In my book, *Another Mother Tongue: Gay Words, Gay Worlds*, I devote an entire chapter to the many stories connecting the color purple to Gay themes, stories of both male and female homosexual lovers.[13] The chapter cites other themes describing purple as the color of Gay shamanic/priesthoods of ancient tribes. It is the most highly spiritual color of the sacred and occult world itself, often a Gay province in human cultures that have not suppressed it. Purple, lavender, the amethyst and amaranth, the violet, the pansy and the hyacinth all figure in Gay stories. Not surprisingly these purple references are also associated with Gay gods, Artemis the hunter, for instance, Apollo and his lover Hyacinthus, and others. This gives me a special way to identify with Sappho's poignant description *Like the hyacinth which shepherds tread underfoot and on the ground the purple flower. . .*[14]

That she bonded with women, then, and worshipped forces described with homosexual (as well as heterosexual) themes, that her lavender-flowered island itself was a center for the sacredness of female bonding, are important to understanding her tradition, and ours. Her gods are part of her intact culture. She called them to her in person, and she addressed them in dream: *I spoke to you in a dream*, she says of Aphrodite. She welcomes Aphrodite to come to her own special orchard, where cold water babbles through apple branches, the altar is smoking with incense, and the whole place is shadowed in roses. How very female a place this is.

Artemis, Sappho says, lives unwed in the wild mountains, and Love, loosener of limbs, never comes near her. Gods and men alike call her the *(virgin, shooter of deer), huntress, a great title*.[15]

In a culture whose prime product was fine wine, Sappho's gods pour from golden cups and jugs golden libations, nectars and wines for each other with great frequency. There is no fear of death, in Sappho's mind. The land beyond death is flower-covered, too. She sometimes craves it, she says, *I get no pleasure from being above the earth, and a longing grips me to die and see the dewy, lotus-covered banks of Acheron*.[16] This death is not oblivion, nor is it the same as the Christian heaven. It is more like the spirit world described by tribal people, a dream that exists next to this one, through which the gods and spirits pass back and forth with messages and mysteries. Immortality was assured to Sappho because her dream is a true one. *Someone, I say, will remember us in the future*,[17] she is confident. The only death is detachment from the dream, from the myth, from the House of the Muses. The woman who does that, Sappho says, who has no share in their roses, will wander all through her poor death among corpses, unseen, *flown from our midst*, and no one will remember her or long for her at all.[18] *That* is death, the only possible one. All else is a continuation of expressive, passionate, lovely and loving life.

Far and away the major theme of Sappho's work is Love, love as manifested in the form of the great Aphrodite or as her servant, Eros. Love, Sappho says, is a tale-weaver, and also bitter-sweet, a snare, a "limb-loosener." Sappho's Love god is sexual and aesthetic, sacred and profane, profound and trivial. Persuasion aids Aphrodite in gaining love for the mortals, and clearly trickery also figures in. I am going to assume that Sappho's Aphrodite was a goddess of intelligence, aesthetic balance and vision as well as of beauty and love. I believe this because there is no reason not to; her world was not severely fragmented, as ours has become.

There is no indication of the terrible division we have been taught to make between the physical and the spiritual, between the body and the mind, between the sexual and the sacred, between beauty and the beast. Consider for a moment the role of dimwit that the greatest symbol of Love and Beauty of our culture, Marilyn Monroe, was forced to play — in spite of her desperate desire to be respected for her acting, for her intellect, for her desire to write poetry. She played a dumb, empty-headed shell of a person, for the benefit of the men who said this was the entirety of their idea of "beauty."

When the apple of female-bonding has shrivelled and is hidden from sight, when the island of female centrality is out of reach, has sunk like Atlantis, and when the Houses of Women speaking common language are silenced, alienation is all that can follow. For women are central to society. When we are split from that centrality and integrity, all society splinters and suffers.

And now, keeping in mind the memory of Aphrodite as a complex Lady with thousands of attributes, let us leave Sappho in her nearly buried world and go on through the loss of the old gods to their possible reclamation in our modern Lesbian poetry. For in looking at our gods, at the spiritual elements and the underlying mythic dreams indigenous to our poetry we can tell something about the integrity of the work and its relation to the movement of feminism, Lesbian feminism and the female culture it represents, that I believe is straining to recoup its highest apple.

The Heaven of Dickinson's Drama

Emily Dickinson worked out, in poetic form, a one-sided dialogue with, virtually an argument with, the god of her father's house, sometimes finding his love enough and other times challenging it with the strength of her own love. Her own love was primarily for women, for the natural elements, and for the "heaven" she sought. Her heaven would be the joining of women, complete in their quality of "queens," and together with each other in a world far different from the constricted one of Amherst where she lived as such an eccentric, brilliant, angry wraith.

> "Heaven" — is what I cannot reach!
> The Apple on the Tree—
> Provided it do hopeless — hang —
> That — "Heaven" is — to Me!
>
> The Color, on the Cruising Cloud —
> The interdicted Land —
> Behind the Hill — the House behind —
> There — Paradise — is found!
>
> Her teasing Purples — Afternoons —
> The credulous — decoy —
> Enamored — of the Conjuror —
> That spurned us — Yesterday![19]

The poem is obviously based on Sappho's sweet-apple reddening on the bough-top.

Interdicted means prohibited, forbidden, "The interdicted land behind the hill, the house behind; there — paradise is found," so Emily described the Lesbian place, a place of "teasing purples" where the old female apple hangs (still helpless) on the tree, for "heaven is what I cannot reach!" In one poem she is explicit that the heaven she envisions is not the Christian one of her father:

> Peruse how infinite I am
> To no one that You — know —
> And sigh for lack of Heaven — but not
> The Heaven God bestow — [20]

Heaven for Emily had a female base. Writing as a woman, she expressed a competitive stance towards the love of Jesus,

> So well that I can live without —
> I love thee — then How well is that?
> As well as Jesus?
> Prove it to me
> That He — loved Men —
> As I — love thee — [21]

Perhaps it was the very impossibility of her poetry really reaching a public audience in her lifetime that enabled her, alone in her room and in her private packets of paper, to so boldly confront the god of the fathers, to challenge his claim to omnipotence. Her poetry expresses open longing for a different kind of heaven. She speaks of time, of death and of longing for love in the same epic terms as any mystic, while living there in the house of her Calvinist father who did not believe in dreams, in art, and who had no use for poetry nor even for books.

> God is indeed a jealous God —
> He cannot bear to see
> That we had rather not with Him
> But with each other play.[22]

What the suffering of the unrequited female love she apparently pined for, could buy, she indicated with this Christian imagery:

> Each was to each The Sealed Church,
> Permitted to commune this — time —
> . . . .

And so when all the time had leaked,
Without external sound
Each bound the Other's Crucifix —

We gave no other Bond —

Sufficient troth, that we shall rise —
Deposed — at length, the Grave —
To that new Marriage,
        Justified — through Calvaries of Love — [23]

She is literally calling for marriage beyond the grave, a new marriage and a new love — which I take to be Lesbian love — justified
by the suffering for its loss. Repeatedly she looked to the future, to
life beyond the grave, as a possible place to enact the marriage of
two queens. That she was keenly aware of a "lost past" that needs
to be restored is stunningly evident in this argument with the patriarchal god:

If "God is Love" as he admits
We think that he must be
Because he is a "jealous God"
He tells us certainly

If "All is possible with" him
As he besides concedes
He will refund us finally
Our confiscated Gods — [24]

A rich variety of colors recur in Dickinson's metaphors drawn
from the natural world of meadows, gardens and landscapes she
daily witnessed in Amherst. But no color occurs more frequently
than does the classic Gay color, purple. She uses purple, violets,
and the stone amethyst repeatedly in her poems. Purple is "the
color of a Queen,"[25] she says in one poem, and we know she used
"Queen" to indicate the fulfilled woman, especially when there are
two queens together.

The following is a poem that perfectly describes her experience of gaining and then losing a woman's love:

I held a Jewel in my fingers —
And went to sleep —
The day was warm, and winds were prosy —
I said, "'Twill keep" —
I woke — and chid my honest fingers
The Gem was gone —
And now, an Amethyst remembrance
Is all I own — [26]

The poem was written about the period of time when Kate Scott wrote her a letter apparently breaking off as hopeless their intensely passionate two-year relationship. The major themes of lost love and of a possible heaven consisting of reuniting, of at last being two queens together, recurred throughout Dickinson's work, apparently constructed of the love she had for Kate Scott, and more consistently, for Sue Gilbert Dickinson.

Emily Dickinson was influenced by the teachings of the more formal Transcendentalists of her time. Their mystic and idealistic beliefs stressed the intuition of the individual rather than logic and externally imposed structures, and stated that an "Oversoul" connects us to natural life on earth and the rest of the universe. Even more, pure metaphysics shines through in this poem on the nature of mortality, the illusion that is our notion of death. She herself, as the poet, knows we live in a long deathless dream, a "Drama" as she calls it:

We dream — it is good we are dreaming —
It would hurt us — were we awake —
But since it is playing — kill us,
And we are playing — shriek —

What harm? Men die — externally —
It is a truth — of Blood —
But we — are dying in Drama —
And Drama — is never dead —

Cautious — We jar each other —
And either — opens the eyes —
Lest the Phantasm — prove the Mistake —
And the livid Surprise

Cool us to Shafts of Granite —
With just an Age — and Name —
And perhaps a phrase in Egyptian —
It is prudenter — to dream — [27]

The "Drama" here is possibly something similar to Sappho's House of the Muses — if we unhook from it, we will fall out of the myth and "cool. . .to Shafts of Granite — / With just an Age — and Name — " become simply historic and material — and finite. Drama, she says is never dead. The poem is so complex and so ahead of her time that I had to learn about Eric Berne's "Game Theory" of psychology *and* read Jane Roberts' messages from Seth, to understand it.

From Drama to a "Real Dream"

To my knowledge, Amy Lowell did not preoccupy herself with the re-establishment of the lost female godhead except indirectly through descriptions of her lover that compared her to a god, or at any rate said that her shawl, "the colour of red violets — / Flares out behind you in great curves / Like the swirling draperies of a painted Madonna."[28] More amusingly, more bitingly, and more essentially erotic/sacred, she wrote this one:

Venus Transiens

Tell me,
Was Venus more beautiful
Than you are,
When she topped
The crinkled waves,
Drifting shoreward
On her plaited shell?

Was Botticelli's vision
Fairer than mine;
And were the painted rosebuds
He tossed to his lady,
Of better worth
Than the words I blow about you
To cover your too great loveliness
As with a gauze
Of misted silver?
for me,
You stand poised
In the blue and buoyant air,
Cinctured by bright winds,
Treading the sunlight.
And the waves which preceed you
Ripple and stir
The sands at my feet[29].

Hilda Doolittle concerned herself with little else than describing the power of female godhead, although the thin amount of attention she has received in anthologies has focussed on her most trivial poems. Supposed to illustrate the form of "imagism," these poems constitute the very smallest part of what she was doing. It is her content, the unfolding epic female content of her fully developed work that marks her as a great poet.

In keeping with being herself a beautiful woman who spent much of her life defining the nature of love, she had complete identification with Helen, goddess of beauty, who is the equivalent, for the European-based culture, of Aphrodite. H.D. wrote much of her work after experiencing the ravishing period of the World Wars. (She and her longtime lover Bryher daringly and typically moved to London during the 200 day *blitzkrieg* in order to see for themselves what was happening to their civilization.) H.D. took as subject the war at Troy, the war that saw Helen fall from power as the queen and god she had been prior to that time. In the "The Walls Do Not Fall," H.D. spoke out of her poetical reality of London wracked with bombing, as all civilization trembled in the

West, and men came home altered from the corpse field and the giant factories of death.

In *Helen in Egypt*, H.D. relives the war of Troy, taking the unique position that Helen was not there, only a dream of Helen walked the ramparts, only an illusion, an empty sleeve, a scarf. The real Helen, she said, was in Egypt all that time, in the occult land of her origin; she was on an island having dialogues with Achilles and other figures from the war. And by removing Helen from the war, from her downfall and death, from her own *loss*, H.D. is saying she can still be found, and found intact. In the occult and Hermetic and other ancient traditions, Helen as a god lives still, love as intelligence lives still, and can be found.

One of the finest sources of that knowledge, H.D. says in one angry poem, is in language itself, and in the work of poets. For we are actually "bearers of the secret wisdom." She says for critics to say that "poets are useless" or "pathetic" —

. . . .
this is the new heresy;
but if you do not even understand what words say,

how can you expect to pass judgment
on what words conceal?

yet the ancient rubrics reveal that
we are back at the beginning:

you have a long way to go,
walk carefully, speak politely

to those who have done their worm-cycle,
for gods have been smashed before

and idols and their secret is stored
in man's very speech,

in the trivial or
the real dream. . . . [30]

In the "real dream" H.D. described seeing the female god, probably in a vision. H.D. was extremely visionary, even to the point of being considered psychotically so, having had five "psy-chotic" episodes in her life for which she was sometimes hospital-ized. Her description of the goddess at the end of the following poem seems extremely realistic to me, not at all a metaphor, or reference (as the beginning of the poem is) to other descriptions from literature but to the memory of someone seen:

> We have seen her
> the world over,
>
> Our Lady of the Goldfinch,
> Our Lady of the Candelabra,
>
> Our Lady of the Pomegranate,
> Our Lady of the Chair;
>
> we have seen her, an empress,
> magnificient in pomp and grace,. . .
>
> the painters did very well by her;
> it is true, they missed never a line
>
> of the suave turn of the head
> or subtle shade of lowered eye-lid
>
> or eye-lids half-raised; you find
> her everywhere (or did find),
>
> in cathedral, museum, cloister,
> at the turn of the palace stair. . .
>
> But none of these, none of these
> suggest her as I saw her,. . .
>
> For I can say truthfully,
> her veils were *white as snow,*
>
> *so as no fuller on earth*
> *can white them;* I can say
>
> she looked beautiful, she looked lovely,
> she was *clothed with a garment*

down to the foot, but it was not
girt about with a golden girdle,

there was no gold, no colour,
there was no gleam in the stuff

nor shadow of hem or seam,
as it fell to the floor; she bore

none of her usual attributes;
the Child was not with her.[31]

Purple, violets, amaranth and similar references to high spiritual content recur in H.D.'s work, as is true of Sappho's fragments, and Emily Dickinson's poems. In one remarkable poem that seems to be on the subject Lesbian love, "Amaranth," H.D. speaks in Sappho's voice directly to Aphrodite:

Am I blind alas,
am I blind,
I too have followed her path.

I too have bent at her feet.
I too have wakened to pluck
amaranth in the straight shaft,
amaranth purple in the cup,
scorched at the edge to white. . .

Ah no — though I stumble toward
her altar-step,
though my flesh is scorched and rent,
shattered, cut apart,
and slashed open;
though my heels press my own wet life
black, dark to purple,
on the smooth rose-streaked
threshold of her pavement. . . . [32]

She ends in Aphrodite's voice:

Turn if you will from her path
for one moment seek
a lesser beauty
and a lesser grace,
but you will find
no peace in the end
save in her presence.[33]

In her intense explorations on the nature of love, H.D. made a remarkable discovery early on, in 1919, when she described a different kind of intelligence than had been previously defined, a "lovemind," she wrote in her journal, a "wombmind." This is from *Notes on Thought and Vision:*

> Vision is of two kinds — vision of the womb and vision of the brain.
>
> In vision of the brain, the region of consciousness is above and about the head; when the center of consciousness shifts and the jelly-fish is in the body, (I visualize it in my case lying on the left side with the streamers or feelers floating up toward the brain) we have vision of the womb or love-vision.
>
> The majority of dream and of ordinary vision is vision of the womb. . . .
>
> The brain and the womb are both centres of consciousness, equally important.[34]

"The brain and the womb are both centres of consciousness, equally important," what a marvelous idea! It is, in fact, a remarkably tribal idea, to say nothing of the tradition of the occult. Not until a well-developed "women's spirituality movement" emerged in the 1970's has there been much possibility of this idea taking root in contemporary society, or of H.D.'s work at last being understood by others than mystics and poets, her peers. She described the circumstances under which one could activate this "lovemind," saying that men could use the "love region" of their bodies in the absence of a womb.

We must be "in love" before we can understand the
mysteries of vision.
A lover must choose one of the same type of mind as
himself, a musician, a musician, a scientist, a
scientist, a general, a young man also interested in the
theory and practice of arms and armies.
We begin with sympathy of thought.
The minds of the two lovers merge, interact in sympathy
of thought.
The brain, inflamed and excited by this interchange of
ideas, takes on its character of over-mind, becomes (as I
have visualized in my own case) a jelly-fish, placed over
and about the brain.
The love-region is excited by the appearance or beauty of
the loved one, its energy not dissipated in physical
relation, takes on its character of mind, becomes this
womb-brain or love-brain that I have visualized as
a jelly-fish *in* the body.
The love-brain and over-brain are both capable of
thought.
This thought is vision.
All men [Author's note: by which she means all people]
have possibilities of developing this vision.[35]

She developed her visualization of the "jelly-fish" of consciousness of the brain and love-minds, she says, just prior to the birth of
her child in March of 1919. She had undergone five years of stultifying unhappiness. Her first marriage, to Richard Aldington, was
destroyed bitterly during the Great War that was one experience
for men and another for women. Her body was torn by a miscar-
riage; during her second pregnancy, doctors predicted death for
herself and her child. She sank into a pervasive depression that left
her dulled and indifferent, apparently dying (though actually
going through a transformation) in a dingy boardinghouse. There,
the young, willful, loyal, completely-in-love Bryher found her and
woke her to new feelings. The daughter of a shipping magnate,

Bryher had the personal capacity to inherit and run the company. Instead, as the daughter, she turned her willfulness towards her own writing and towards supporting innovative writers around her, James Joyce, for example, and especially H.D. (though H.D. actually had plenty of money of her own). Bryher, who was Jewish, spent her money on liberal causes, and got several people out of Nazi Germany. She was apparently scorned — probably jealously — by male admirers of H.D.'s extraordinary beauty. Bryher's later photographs show a butchy woman with extremely short hair wearing man-type suits. H.D. described her small, strange companion as a little gray gull, an elf.

> That's life,
> but I had grown accustomed
> to disapppointment,
> insecurity, gloom;
>
> I begged for a place in their room
> I, a shadow, sought a place
> where disgrace attended. . .
>
> O what, what, what
>
> sent you, all grey, unnoticeable
> and small
> to shatter my peace,
> unconscionable little gull?[36]

Bryher took her to the Scilly Islands off Cornwall and in July, just weeks after their relationship began, H.D. wrote her remarkable descriptions of the "love-mind." The new understanding of vision happened to her, she said, just prior to the birth of her child; that is, just as Bryher entered her life. It is a special mind, a mind of vision that could best be entered, she said, by like-minded people. Her examples imply love between homosexual men, for what other relationship during that time would involve a general and a soldier? She does not explicitly name a Lesbian pair bond, yet "writer with writer" describes herself and Bryher, and it was certainly during the first excitement of their love-bond that her insights about the "love-brain" came to her — perhaps in some such circumstances as is described in this poem from her series on Bryher, "Halcyon." (A halcyon is a special bird that calms stormy seas. The word means happy, tranquil and idyllic.)

> You say, "lie still";
> your hand is chill,
> cold, unimpassioned,
> inviolable;
>
> you say, "lie back,
> you won't faint";
> what makes you think that?
> what makes you think
>
> I won't drift out,
> get quite away?. . . . [37]

Quarreling was a great part of the feelings let loose by the emotionally-awakened H.D., and she ends "Halcyon" with this:

> . . . .
> we quarrel again —
> don't talk—dismiss happiness,
> unhappiness, pain, bliss,
> even thought—
>
> what's left?
> imcomparable beyond belief,
> white stones
> immaculate sand,
>
> the slow move-forward of the tide
> on a shallow reef,
> salt and dried weed,
> the wind's low hiss;

it's here in my skull
(leave your hand there)
for you—for ever—
mysterious little gull.[38]

It's clear from her poetry that what H.D. sought and got from Bryher was a steadfast foundation in reality. From this island she reached into the deepest levels of the "real dream," finding there an old female god of love, beauty, intelligence and vision.

Gods from Tribal Worlds

As early as 1970, Audre Lorde began pulling godstuff from the African and Afro-American traditions into her work. In "The Winds of Orisha," she begins, "This land will not always be foreign."[39] The poem speaks of Tiresias, the Greek figure who "took 500 years to grow into a woman / so do not despair of your sons." It then continues with descriptions of the major Macumba gods, who are called the "Orisha:" Yemanja, Oshun, Oya, Shango, and Eshu. This pantheon was retained in North and South America by Black slaves who mixed the religion with some American Indian gods and customs, then, in Brazil especially, coated it all with a thin Catholic veneer for camouflage:

. . . Mother Yemanja raises her breasts to begin my labor
near water
the beautiful Oshun and I lie down together
in the heat of her body truth my voice comes stronger
Shango will be my brother roaring out of the sea
earth shakes our darkness swelling into each other
warming winds will announce us living
as Oya, Oya my sister my daughter
destroys the crust of the tidy beaches
and Eshu's black laughter turns up the neat sleeping
sand.[40]

109

Eshu is the eternal trickster of the crossroads, highly phallic and somewhat resembling American Indian Coyote and ancient tribal Hermes in his raucous and chaotic functions of disrupting the fixed order of belief. Yemanja is the Great Mother of the Sea; Oshun is Beauty, the Evening Star and inland waters, the lake. Oya, to whom Lorde devoted another full poem on the subject of anger, and who she calls "my sister my daughter," is the storm goddess, a warrior supreme, unafraid of the spirits of the dead. Her brother is Shango, who received his tools, his Thor-like battle ax, from her.

I believe it was following a trip Lorde made to Africa in the early or mid-seventies that she added to these Yoruba gods from a second African-based pantheon, the Vodu from Dahomey, or Dan, as the ancient, powerful culture center was called formerly.

Gods of both regions constitute the group she prays to and through in *The Black Unicorn*. In these poems she successfully transfers them to New York streets and sees them in the persons of modern urban Americans in a manner similar to that used by Sappho when she describes the qualities of love and beauty in the persons of women she loves. Similarly, the American Indian poet Joy Harjo acknowledges the deity of the Moon by seeing her in a bar in Albuquerque;[41] and in *The Queen of Wands*, I locate Helen in a factory and as a factory. The point is that deity does not live in the remote heavens, nor stay hidden and exclusive in cloisters and grottoes no matter how appealing. The godpower must come out and be present with us where we are, where we live and act and feel, here in concrete and plastic, in airplanes and freeways and tenements and brutality and cancer and chemical addictions and need and threat of nuclear war. Here is where we shall find, locate and establish the gods to help us on this continent of mixtures and dishevelment to help them feel at home.

Audre Lorde addresses her gods forcefully and naturally, as in "125th Street and Abomey" (Abomey is the capital of Dahomey):

Head bent, walking through snow
I see you Seboulisa
printed inside the back of my head. . .
Seboulisa mother goddess with one breast
eaten away by worms of sorrow and loss
see me now
your severed daughter
laughing our name into echo
all the world shall remember.[42]

Like Paula Gunn Allen with her Indian traditions, Lorde is able to translate the details of her life into mythic terms. For instance in "From the House of Yemanja":

My mother had two faces and a frying pot
where she cooked up her daughters
into girls
before she fixed our dinner.
My mother had two faces
and a broken pot
where she hid out a perfect daughter
who was not me. . . [43]

Of particular importance to the work of understanding and developing a new Lesbian archetype is Lorde's surfacing with the Black woman warrior, of whom she names several. The storm god Oya we have met, with her thunders and her winds and rain. Afrikete is most well developed in Lorde's biomythography, *Zami*; Afrikete is a trickster, a changer, a mysterious and lavish lover, a singer and a poet. Colossa is a dancer, appearing in the poem "Scar" as a "big black woman with jewels in her eyes. . . her head in a golden helmet/arrogant/plumed. . . / her thighs are like stanchions. . . " and at the shiny edge of her metal tunic, "an astonishment of black curly hair."[44]

And finally, "The Women of Dan Dance with Swords in Their Hands to Mark the Time When They Were Warriors," is both the name of a poem and a description of the line of African Amazons who served the Panther Kings of Dahomey. In her American context and in Lorde's hands, the old African Amazon is a unification of anger and love, resolution and affirmation, transformed purposefully out of the slave/servant times:

. . .
I do not come like a secret warrior
with an unsheathed sword in my mouth
hidden behind my tongue
slicing my throat to ribbons
of service with a smile
while the blood runs down and out
through holes in the two sacred mounds
on my chest.

I come like a woman
who I am
spreading out through nights
laughter and promise
and dark heat
warming whatever I touch
that is living consuming
only
what is already dead.[45]

By connecting her life, and by extension all of our lives, to the ancient and still underlying tribal life, to the communitas of rite and of gods, Lorde is helping us to gain meaning on a plane far greater than the everyday drudge of physical activity. Dickinson called this entering the "Drama, and Drama never dies." Sappho called it being connected to the House of the Muses, and that those who failed to do so would be forgotten, even among the dead. H.D. called it the "real dream." Lorde calls it "our name," and "memory," messages brought to us through the magic office and voice of a special contemporary unicorn, the Black unicorn.

Having a mythic history with genuine godforces operating on a daily level is completely necessary to the Lesbian poetic search for what Mary Carruthers calls a new Lesbian *civitas*, a paradigm, a model of a new community, a new relationship of women to the world.

Sappho had an integrated religious ceremonial/mythological matrix to draw from, one shared by all her audience, not only a "common language" with common dreams, but also with common gods. Our tradition is fragmented, actually fractured, and each of the Lesbian poets of our era is drawing from a completely different tradition for her naming and defining of her gods. Even Olga Broumas, a native Greek, who naturally draws from the Greek mythology of her land of origin, alters the stories so drastically as to be unrecognizable to Sappho's ancient unencumbered world. But Broumas' act is necessary for the restructuring, for the old tales have been dissembled to the disadvantage of women and of tribal beings. Broumas is in the tradition of Sappho, therefore, when she re-feminizes and revitalizes the old names, as in "Twelve Aspects of God" wherein all twelve are female — Circe, Demeter, Artemis, Calypso. Here is the second part of "Amazon Twins:"

> In the gazebo-like cafe, you gave
> me food from your plate, alert
> to my blood-sweet hungers
> double edged
> in the glare of the sun's
> and our own
> twin heat. Yes, there
> we were, breasts on each side, Amazons
> adolescent at twentynine
> privileged
> to keep the bulbs and to feel the blade
> swell, breath-sharp
> on either side. In that public place
>
> in that public place.[46]

113

Caritas and *Beginning With O* define a Lesbian sexuality that is sacred, aware, has a mythic history and is totally present. As critic Mary Carruthers puts it:

> Innocence, play, sentience, and familiarity are the marks of Broumas' erotic language. Her love poetry desires not *raptus*, the loss of self, but depicts union through recognition, through images of choir, dance, laughter, touch, of diverse yet familiar voices making sweet harmony. The tongue, organ of speech and consciousness, which in romantic tradition is opposite and inadequate to the desired unconscious *raptus* of sexual union, is in this new context an instrument both of sex and consciousness. In that fortunate Lesbian correspondence, Broumas lays the foundation of her myth. . . [47]

And in her myth god is female, is varied, is familiar, and is sapphically erotic, as in "Innocence," where the poet finds,

> with the glide of a tongue, a hand
> precise as an eyelid, a hand with a sense
> of smell, a hand that will dance
> to its liquid moan.
> God's hand. . . [48]

In a later book, *Pastoral Jazz*, a book that never fails to give me some happiness, Broumas has gone into a subterranean level, a starting over that repeats the sensation of something beautiful, sad, and fierce that is busy being born of a shallow green sea with lavender shadows. "The child goes underground, whirling and fainting," she says in "Sea Change."[49]

Broumas in *Pastoral Jazz* is no longer naming, she is unnaming. Naming and re-naming are only two of our chores. Another is unnaming, as is found in Gertrude Stein, Paula Gunn Allen, and in my own "She Who" poems and novel, *The Motherlords*. *Pastoral*

Jazz leaves both name and story behind to enter language, still erotic, as everything Broumas' pen touches is infused with Lesbian sexuality and a female aesthetic that is holy, and wholly physical.

> Delta and Delta to the touch
> Nile streaming *open open*
> Open of opens
> which sun sings? which sea
> stiff nippled curly measures?[50]

In poetry of language and the body, what is imparted is impression and essential rhythm, as when birds talk. What is imparted is no longer rigid, defined, structured, superimposed, or mandatory. It is *calling* rather than naming; and the emotions can include delight, humor, and the sublimely ludicrous as well as the seriously beautiful, the sexual and the sacred.

In this scheme, small things are what matters:

> No choice but a gradual ascent, the silkworm's
> passage to Byzantium from China, deliberate loss of all
> heroism, even in pleasure. Hammock cords
> shake in the light. You sit down
> to a common meal, raw carrots,
> lettuce, radishes, olives and other things, a place
> both empty and set.[51]

And in this scheme, Venus is always being re-born from the sea, everything is beginning, and the apple is found to have seeds:

> If I think along
> the stations of the day
> how observe them?
> Sweet apples
> Mild chill of fall
> harvested and resown seeds
> Always to be beginning![52]

Godmind, Godforce, Godlove

None of the Lesbian poets under discussion concentrate on one female divinity, as in the sense of "The Goddess," or even, "The Mother," and write to her; all of us are pantheistic.

Yet even calling Adrienne Rich "pantheistic" may seem absurd given that she has never, to my knowledge, named in the magic of her poetry a female god, or addressed her, or even mentioned her in passing. And yet she names the forces, the female godforces, and takes as her major subjects love and beauty, intelligence and memory — surely Aphrodite or perhaps the Hebrew Asherah — in another form. Moreover, Rich writes, like the rest of us, in a metaphysical time frame, sure sign of a seer connected to what occultists and spiritualists call "the higher mind," the one that is eons old, the one with the long and sacred memory.

Speaking out of the mouth of the brilliant painter Paula Becker, who died in childbirth in 1907, Rich says:

> . . . . I have the feeling I'm
> moving somewhere, patiently, impatiently,
> in my loneliness. I'm looking everywhere in nature
> for new forms, old forms in new places,
> the planes of an antique mouth, let's say, among the
> leaves.
> I know and do not know
> what I am searching for.[53]

And in "Nights and Days" she has her eye on a certain flower, a hyacinth (was it the one Sappho said the shepherds trampled in the mountains, twenty-five hundred years ago?). "The stars will come out over and over / the hyacinths rise like flames / from the windswept turf down the middle of upper Broadway" — this hyacinth is located in the center of the city; she continues,

> We are holding hands so I can see
> everything as you see it

I follow you into your dreams
your past, the places
none of us can explain to anyone.[54]

And then she describes the lover's sleep as "sacred." The sun
is female, the city is "wrapped in her indestructible light." The
poem "Sibling Mysteries" is a chronicle of the recognition of two
sisters recalling the long history of women as the daughters of the
mother: "piecing our lore in quilted galaxies."[55] And, so beautifully in "Twenty-One Love Poems," she describes the godspirit as
"nameless till we rename her:"

XI

Every peak is a crater. This is the law of volcanoes,
making them eternally and visibly female.
No height without depth, without a burning core,
though our straw soles shred on the hardened lava.
I want to travel with you to every sacred mountain
smoking within like the sibyl stooped over her tripod,
I want to reach for your hand as we scale the path,
to feel your arteries glowing in my clasp,
never failing to note the small, jewel-like flower
unfamiliar to us, nameless till we rename her,
that clings to the slowly altering rock —
that detail outside ourselves that brings us to ourselves,
was here before us, knew we would come, and sees beyond
us.[56]

Each of the contemporary Lesbian poets has drawn from the myth
of an "ideal place," a new island from which to center a civilized,
graceful loving culture that has passion and physical substance as
well as metaphysical and psychic substance. In Lorde's work, this
ideal place is sometimes "Dahomey," or even more anciently,
"Dan." In Broumas, it is the sea, as well as the lovers' arms, a place
of continual rebirth. Sappho used Lesbos as an ideal place, speaking of the poets of Lesbos as the best and herself as best of the best.

In her newest poem, "Sources," Adrienne Rich locates an ideal place from a Jewish context:

XXI

YERUSHALAYIM: a vault of golden heat
hard-pulsing from bare stones

the desert's hard-won, delicate green
the diaspora of the stars

thrilling like thousand-year-old locusts
audible yet unheard

a city on a hill
waking with first light to voices

piercing, original, intimate
as if my dreams mixed with the cries

of the oldest, earliest birds
and of all whose wrongs and rights

cry out for explication
as the night pales and one more day

breaks on this *Zion* of hope and fear
and broken promises

                                  this promised land[57]

Each poet has located the place of wholeness and the method of approaching it — each location is specific to the background, ethnicity and experience of the poet, yet each place applies as well to all people. Yerushalayim is Rich's Jewish/American metaphor for "the city on the hill," the ideal civilization. And the "diaspora of the stars," is not only a reference to the Jewish diaspora, the scattering of Hebrew tribes from the original place, it is also the scattering of all our tribal beings, all our memory of our own tribes, of dreams, become — not ashes — but stars. Stars. Hopes. Worlds. Renewals.

As for the godstuff in my own work, the "She Who" poems were the first of my poems that I thought of as *conjure* poems. I think of them as that because not only are they using strongly physical imagery, they are also using strong rhythms that call the thing to itself with images and sounds. They were deliberately aimed at a physical part of the body, to trigger a particular response in the human body. I knew I was getting the words close to the feeling/state I wanted to conjure for each poem if a little gland in my throat went off when I read the poem to myself — a little spit gland, probably, with a sharp pang attached to it. If this gland went off, I knew the poem was a finished "She Who" poem and I added it to the stack.

I did not know about chakras at that time, the little energy wheels whirling at certain parts of our bodies — the tailbone area, sexual area, solar plexus, heart, throat, third eye, and top of the head. Probably the little throat gland that I aimed the "She Who" poems at is the physical correlative of the throat chakra. Like Gertrude Stein, I was attempting to surround the subject of female godforce without naming it. In 1972 when the series was written, the Lesbian feminist movement was nearly completely materialist in its orientation. Besides, hadn't I spent years scorning spirituality?

Additionally, I would not have known what name to use; I have never liked the word goddess because it seems to be a diminutive of the word "god" and not an active principle on its own account. I recognize hundreds of forces, spirits, shadows, gods, goblins, and fairies, as well as major female and male gods who, in my life, have taken a variety of forms. I cannot imagine consolidating all that variety of form and pulse into monotheism.

But in "Confrontations With The Devil In The Form of Love," Love is personified in a direct manner, and "the Devil" is a form of Sappho, of women's fractured sexual being, and by extension the whole sunken antique tribal world that underlies our Western history, that has been burnt and misshapen.

My name is Judith, meaning
She Who Is Praised
I do not want to be called praised
I want to be called The Power of Love.

if Love means protect then whenever I do not
defend you
I cannot call my name Love.
if Love means rebirth then when I see us
dead on our feet
I cannot call my name Love
if Love means provide & I cannot
provide for you
why would you call my name Love?[58]

The re-naming of Love is brought foreward most strongly in "A Woman Is Talking To Death." There, the "death-myth" of the old patriarchal system is juxtaposed to the ability of any kinds of "lovers" to defend each other against it, and to band together in another place:

we are the fat of the land, and
we all have our list of casualties

to my lovers I bequeath
the rest of my life. . . . [59]

In the "Confrontations" poem, "My name is Judith," the re-naming of Love involves calling for its power out in the world, a power not yet realized ("do not mistake my breasts for mounds of potatoes. . . nor take my feet to be acres of solid brown earth").[60] Most importantly, don't mistake for "romance" the Love the poet is asking us all to seek. Don't mistake Love for escape, for the security of the couple bond that compensates for all we do not have of love and autonomy, of choice and definition, of power and the sacredness of our beings, in the world at large. Let us take on the world at large, and recreate these things within it. Love is being named now, in

120

these poems, poems which mock Love's fall from power as merely
Venus, the headless body of a statue:

> Venus dear, where are your arms?
> if only you were a tree.
> they have so many
> & no one thinks less of them for it.[61]

Love is being named, personified, and confronted with the
limitations that have been placed on her, is being asked to become
more, much much more. She is being openly addressed, as Aphrodite was openly addressed by Sappho, but here she has an
American name, an Anglo-Saxon name, Love. Her powers are her
"apples." She has a different history, has been a "devil," has been a
sex-toy, a Venus, has been "simply romance."[62] As this "Devil,"
which is less-than-herself, she is being confronted in the poems.
She is being asked to transform her functions now, to include protection, provision and power, and to be out in the world with us,
as our partner.

Love, combined with intelligence and beauty, at last joined
together in my poetry and in my understanding in *The Queen of
Wands*. Adrienne Rich in her introduction to my first collection of
poetry had gotten me interested in a poet I had previously considered too classical for me to understand: H.D.. Between *Helen in
Egypt* and a line of Rich's about "loving with all my intelligence,"
I came to some stories of Helen as a stolen god, a god of creativity
and of the old weaving powers. These female weaving powers have
been deified on this continent as well, in the person of the Pueblo
Indian creatrix, Spider Grandmother. Helen, as the female god of
love, creation, weaving, fire and beauty, is a form of Aphrodite:
beauty as intelligent creativity, love as a form of envisioning,
envisioning with a psychic/sexual mind. The Helen poems in *The
Queen of Wands* place her majesty squarely in the world, the everyday American workaday world, as the "egg of being," the dream of
America itself; and the voice describing her as such is the ancient
tribal one, the deep one underneath in the purple shadows, Spider
Webster.

Helen
you always were
the egg laid
by the golden goose,
the full pot, the fat purse,
the best bet, the sure horse
the Christmas rush
the bundle he's about to make;
the gold mine, a house of our own
the ship come in, the next stake,
the nest egg, the big deal, the steal—
the land of opportunity
the lovely lady being
luck and love and lust
and the last chance
for any of us,
the reason that he's living
for, Helen you're always
high card, ace in the hole and
more, the most, the first and best,
the sun
burst
goodness   quenching every thirst
the girl of the golden golden golden
West,
desire that beats
in every chest

heart of the sky

and some bizarre
dream substance
we pave streets with
here in America[63]

And in that book of poems (which is the first of four books chronicling queens from the Tarot and other sources),

Love/Beauty/Mind in the form of the stolen Helen promises to return in her rightful position as Mother of the People. The second book, *The Queen of Swords*, will undertake definition and re-cognition of the warrior, the quintessential Dyke. From the research I have done, and from knowing the habits of Lesbians, and from understanding that the warrior she-god of ancient and tribal times has been a wielder of storms, and a lover of her powers, I have written the following poem or verse of a poem:

Lesbians love to dance / inside the thunder

Lesbians love to dance
outside in the rain
with lightning darting
all around them. Lesbians
love to dance together
in the pouring rain, in
summer.
Lesbians love to dance
inside the thunder,
sheets of water
washing over their whole bodies
and the dark clouds
boiling and roiling like a
giant voice calling.
Lesbians love to answer
voices calling like that.
Lesbians love to
dance without their clothing
in thunderstorms with
lightning as their partner.
Screaming, holding hands
and turning soaking faces
skyward in tumultuous noise and yearning. Lesbians
love to see each other
learning to completely
rejoice. Lesbians love

to feel the power
and the glory they can dance
inside of, in a storm
of their communal choice.[64]

The pantheon of Paula Gunn Allen, as it has developed in her work, includes the Laguna Pueblo Indian female creator gods, especially Grandmother Spider, who is also called Thought Woman, and her sister, the Mother of the People, Corn Woman or Iyatiku. Allen's "biomythography," to use Audre Lorde's apt word, is *The Woman Who Owned the Shadows*. Stories of the Indian gods, especially female gods, figure prominently, giving the protagonist ways to make a meaning of her life in our fractured modern American society.

Although weaving, especially weaving the universe from her own substance, is a primary quality of Allen's creatrix, water is Allen's major image of grace. Sappho, too, used liquid imagery most often to describe her gods' behaviors. They pour golden nectars and wines, fill cups and jugs, while cold water babbles through apple-branches in the sacred groves. She speaks of dewy banks, of dews shed in beauty, of ambrosia in bowls, and intriguingly, of a dripping wet napkin.

Perhaps it is only natural from a native of the great desert of the Southwest, as Allen is, and a member of a tribe calling itself Laguna, "Lake," that she would say of rain, "so when it rains everyone is whole, you know that god loves you."[65]

Allen uses water in describing her coming out into the world of Lesbianism as it has manifested itself in America for the last decade, and of coming out into a consciousness of the possible bonds and beauty, the possible love and wisdom, of all women. The following lines are from a poem called "He Na Tye Woman" (Female Rain Woman):

Water (woman) that is the essense of you
He na tye (woman) that is recognition and remembering.
Gentle. Soft. Sure.

Water (woman) that is the essense of you
He na tye (woman) that is recognition and remembering.
Gentle. Soft. Sure.
Long shadows of afternoon, growing as the light turns
west toward sleep. Turning with the sun.
(The rest of it is continents and millenia.
(How could I have waited so long for completion?)

The water rises around us like the goddess coming home.
(Arisen.) Some trip, all things considered, all times
and visions, all places and spaces taken into account
on that ancient journey, finally returned. The maps, the
                                                    plans,
the timetables: the carefully guided tours into all manner
of futilities. Manners the last turn in the road: arid irony.

(Lady, why does your love so touch me?
(Lady, why do my hands have strength for you?
(Lady, how could I wander so long without you?

Water in Falls, misting and booming on the rocks below.
Tall pines in the mist, the deep carved caves.
Water in rivulets. Gathering speed, drops joining in
                                                headlong
flight.
Unnamed rivers, flowing eternally underground,
                                    unchanging, unchanged.
Water thundering down long dry arroyos, the ancient
                                                causeways
of our faith. Drought over, at last. Carrying silt,
bits of broken glass, branches, pebbles, pieces of
                                            abandoned cars,
parts of lost houses and discarded dreams. Downstream.
Storms of water, and we
deluged
singing
hair plastered to our ecstatic skulls,

waving wild fists at the bolts hurled at us from above
teeth shimmering in the sheets of rain (the sheen)
eyes blinded with the torrents that fall fromthroughover
them:

Rain. The Rain that makes us new.
That rain is you.
How did I wait so long to drink.[66]

God, at Laguna is female, is Spider Grandmother, Thought
Woman. The legend says that she went away, after the people
stopped following her rituals. In Allen's work she is called forth
again, in a more modern and out-in-the-world form — and
through the bonding of women together. "Recognition and
remembering" are the qualities the "grandlady" god has in He Na
Tye Woman. In "Transitions," the poet makes even more explicit
her return and the place of Lesbian love in her re-calling:
. . . .

how you loved me. made love to me.
what i saw there when i was held.
in the wild tangle of our tongues' necessity,
rooting in softleafed places,
melting and pouring like the hills today,
ground gone to water, running toward the sea,
heat rising but not in rage.
in love.
just the seagray of your gaze,
your longing, arms raised to clasp
me,
     in sight
         of the Woman
  she
       lying in a pond
          in the woods
  in the pond of her self,
           her dreams.
  lying breathless, she
  taken with a dream

a sighting
of her lovely lover
　　　who is coming down,
　　　　　running down
　to meet her where she's waiting
　in her pond, in her lake, in her sea.
we could see her waiting
　　　for the time to be
　　　　　her time.

　her arms ready to rise
　her knees beginning to open, to lift,

we said: she's waking to love.

. . . .

the woman whose waking means
wonder.
water.
want and need.
and her awakening is not death or war, not rage.
she's in love, that woman the world. she's in love.[67]

It is striking to me to realize that none of the gods described, named, addressed in our poetry is omnipotent. Audre Lorde specifies in the notes in *The Black Unicorn* that the Orisha are not omnipotent, are not even always just. Similarly, the gods of Paula Gunn Allen's Indian world always need the participation of the human beings to complete their activity. As Rich says in her description of the flower who is a small detail outside ourselves and has, somehow, always known where we are going—the godstuff, the godhead and the godfoot and the godmind and the godsex and the godlove is within us as well as without us. We are an active, intelligent *part* of what is sacred, even a necessary part, as is everything else.

The feminist spiritual writer, Starhawk, speaks of this definition of deity in her article, "Consciousness, Politics and Magic," in *The Politics of Women's Spirituality*:

Estrangement permeates our society so thoroughly that to us it seems to *be* consciousness itself; even the language for other possibilities has disappeared or been deliberately twisted. Yet, another form of consciousness is possible, indeed, has existed from earliest times. It underlies other cultures and has survived even in the West in hidden streams. This is the consciousness I call *immanence*— the awareness of the world and everything in it as alive, dynamic, interdependent, and interacting, infused with moving energies: a living being, a weaving dance.[68]

Paula Gunn Allen goes even further using a cosmology drawn from American Indian and modern "Sethian" understanding of the physical world as not only alive, but malleable, responding to our expressed desires. Our gods can be seen, she says, by looking at how we order our world, at *what we do*. In a poem, "Taku skanskan," she has put this idea to words:

> that history is an event
> that life is
> that I am event
> ually to go do something
> the metaphor for god.
> eventuality.
> activity.
>
> what happens   *to be*
> what happens   *to me*
> god. history. action.
> the Lakota word for it is:
> *what movesmoves.*
> they don't call god "what moves something."
> not "prime mover,"
> "first mover," "who moves everything or nothing,"
> "action," "lights," or "movement."
> not "where" or "what" or "how," but

event. GOD
is what happens, is:
movesmoves.

riding a mare.
eventuality.
out of the corral into morning
taking her saddled and bridled
air thick with breath movesmoves
horsebreath, mybreath, earthbreath,
skybreathing air. ing.
breathesbreathes   movesmoves
in the cold. winterspringfall.
corral.   ing.   horse and breath.
air. through the gate moveswe.
lift we the wooden crossbar *niya*
movesmoves unlocks movesbreathes
lifebreath of winter soul
swings wide sweet corral gate
happens to be frozenstiff in place
happens to be cold. so I and mare
wear clothes that move in event
of frozen. shaggy hair dressers for the air
breathes breathe we: flows: movesmoves:
god its cold
no other place but movesmoves
horse me gate hinge air bright frost lungs
swing gate out far morning winter rides
movesmovingmoves Lakota words: god.
what we do.[69]

God. What we do. In reclaiming and renaming the "confiscated gods," as Dickinson called them, we are also involving the
reclamation of the "city," civitas, civilization with "caritas," as
Broumas calls love. The place, the placenta, the connection to the
Mother of Everything, as it is called by all of us; the unique and

very female "heaven" of Dickinson; the white island of H.D.'s mind that is not Lesbianism but is a place of the power of women;[70] Laguna the lake of healing waters of Allen; Dahomey the ancient center of Dan of Lorde; Yerushalayim land of promises and broken promises of Adrienne Rich; "the egg of being," the golden dream of America for me — where the egg is the dream immanent and the tree, the weaving tree, is the dream manifested. The place where we can be decent to each other. Where the culture-trance of oppositions is broken. Where there is some measure of safety, though as Rich says, "not anesthesia," not an "insured, guaranteed life." A place where the usual strident, linear oppositions no longer prevail because we shall have made a larger metaphor that incorporates the oppositional one within it. We shall have made a womb, or heart-shaped metaphor.

Describing the New Center

Defining and describing and uncovering a new or restored creation myth is in large measure what we are doing. In her article describing Lesbian poetry, Mary Carruthers says we have moved beyond revolution, into a longer arena, "eschatology," the final end of things — transformation of all things by transforming the words for them. She says,

> Eschatology, however, requires utter change, the end of all things as we know them, a new heaven and a new earth. It is a natural historical perspective for mystics and seers, for all those who by inclination and necessity do not vest their interest wholly in society but remain always in some way apart. The fact of her permanent estrangement is an essential ingredient of the Lesbian myth in its relationship to tradition, history and the poetic process.[71]

What we are doing, she says, is re-mythologizing our society, establishing a new *civitas*, a Lesbian civility, using the image, the metaethic of integrity, wholeness. *Civitas* meant originally the body of the citizens, the community. Only later did it come to mean the physical place, the city, the buildings and the streets. In medieval times, it was the community of believers on earth, with the City of God located in another place, away, in heaven.

The Lesbian *civitas*, community is located here in the world of cold and hot factuality, here in a place that is the fragrant and stinking mother-place; that is, it is here with everything that it is. And it is here in the middle of the current fragmented alienated patriarchal world. But the new *civitas* is here with its spiritual connections intact, here with its mysticism and its forces intact. It is here in bondings with familiars and an overlapping of commonality even in differences; here in a bond of community whose definitions can be indefinitely expanded as long as the principles of central integration, of factuality rather than idealism, and of the centrality of women to herself are kept.

Each of the modern Lesbian poets under discussion proceeds with a very particular process of creating a new mythology. Valuing the bond of Lesbianism, speaking out from it into the modern world, we define origin or homeland as an ideal place. Then, by carrying the modern world into that poetry with us, we place the most extreme and stereotyped female powers of our experience into the exact center of the modern world, infusing them not only with value and history, but with centrality and finally with godhead, immmanence, to use Starhawk's word, and godmind, including "wombmind."

The effect of exchange is uncanny, is transformational. For the procedure produces, or induces, an *inversion*, as though one reached down a coat sleeve and pulled at the sleeve tip, tugging until it reversed, revealing an entirely different pattern and meaning of the coat than the one formerly exposed.

When Adrienne Rich places women in history and Jewish women (as she has done in *Sources*) in the central position of the universe of her poetry, she produces, or induces, from the Chosen People, a new and vibrant *choosing woman*. A woman of choices who takes full responsibility for her choices even when, as in "Phantasia for Elvira Shatayev," they lead to her certain death on a mountain climbing expedition. The consequence of taking responsibility for making choices is that she also takes full responsibility for her powers, for locating and using them. The woman of Rich's poetry emerges out of history as more-than-history, more than singled-out, she becomes selector and judge as well. She is connected to all the natural universe; no longer walking a linear time path only, she can see beyond time. She is no longer split away from the universe, she is integrated with it.

When Olga Broumas places the women of Western traditional myth into sexual relation to each other, explicit and detailed, the formerly degraded mythic sexual being of the female becomes exalted. She is sacred and at the same time tremendously real and present, *god in the flesh*, wet, trembling, alive and right there beside you, inside you, all over your life sharp and warm and painful and demanding and passionate and sacred.

When Audre Lorde takes the traditional American myth that has sealed Blackness in with terror and violence, has tarred and feathered it with threat and supernatural physical powers, when she takes this flint black cutting edge of all our nightmares into the exact center of the universe of her work, giving the woman all the dimensions of her female form, charged with her erotic sensibility of Lesbianism, the result is transformative. The woman who emerges from the boiling pit of racist, misogynist, alienating and very urban America is a warrior who combines anger with love, not conquest, not slaughter, not self-destruction, but anger with love, two-in-one, a "colossa," a very special kind of female warrior who comes from the ideal place of Dan. As such she is a protector, a mother-warrior who has undertaken to use her tongue as a sword, with capacity to slice away the sludge and dross, to warm what is alive and to kill meticulously "what is already dead," leaving a freshly shining place, a surface of "black light." She is a warrior who is protector rather than conqueror. She is also the "destructor" as creator, the anger that prepares a new path. She is the creator who is herself in danger of destruction and who in protecting herself, creates protection for others. In this process of inverting the myth of race in America, "blackness and whiteness," the terror and violence in each of us can resolve into anger, be integrated into our lives and allowed to co-exist with love.

In my work the "common" and the highly charged folk underground of European Gay and female-based tribal cultural values are catapulted into a central position that places power directly into the hands of women, *locates it there*, who have had it torturously usurped as long ago as ten centuries or more. Pervasive passivity is overturned by this return to recognition and centrality of the ancient powers; the woman who emerges from the definition of a life that has been mute, battered and like a pale shadow comes out with courage and joy. The poems call on her to bestir her memory, her mysticism and her claim to powers.

The poems say that this is done simply by willful effort, by the creative force of "work," by resolve and intent, and by staying on this earth, in this life and in touch with facts rather than attempting to escape or deny. What had been seen as common, a dull drudgery, is now seen as beautiful. This is not alienated beauty, a toy or a sterile Aryan weapon dragged from colonial era to colonial era. This is ripe, rich beauty as it is in the universe, the beauty of love as it manifests in the burning and cooling stars that become planets on purpose, as well as butterflies that become worms on purpose, become the substance and relationship of the intelligent, forceful esthetic that is all life.

In Paula Gunn Allen's work, placement of the American Indian as a female in the central position completely alters the patriarchal belief that the Indian people were marauding horseriders living on the fringe of "civilized" society. Allen's work pulls this false idea away like the flimsy justifying curtain that it is, revealing the tribal mother who is actually there. We see, rather than exotic relics of barbaria, the woman (the tribal people, the originators) who is the central provider of all our wealth, our health, and our knowledge of freedom and rights of the individual.

133

The American dream itself lies behind the curtain Allen pulls off for us. The woman who is there is the source; she is the underlying gynarchic network that sustains all the superstructure of industrial life. Nor will the things we value and neglect to value, the live earth, the good food, healing herbs and great continental spaciousness, the crisp, clean air, lovely fierce animals and the essential individual freedoms — nor will they survive our neglect if we neglect and destroy the gynarchic and tribal people who produced them. By recognizing and re-valuing the gynarchic and essentially woman-bonded matrix underlying what we say we treasure, we may yet realize the golden possibility; we may all even see that we, too, came from and can reconstruct such worlds.

Returning to Sappho's Gods

And now, having gone through some history and speculation, description and revelation, it seems appropriate to look once more at Sappho's use of the gods in her work and in her world.

Suppose that in part at least, what the ancients named as gods were highly developed psychic states ("the sleep of enchantment"[72]) achieved through using clear emotions: Aries, anger; Aphrodite, love; Adonis, tragic sorrow. Suppose that, when Sappho said that Aphrodite lives in a golden house, she was describing the way love looks, when we are able to enter the psychic mode of seeing/feeling, as she was. I say that Sappho was able to enter that plane of being because tribal people do; they maintain everyday contact with the spirit world, the world of dream and vision. And we know that along with the destruction of Sappho's work from the ancient world, there has also been suppression of the psychic plane (until recently) and of the erotic dimension of the sacred. The psychic world, incidentally, is accessed most successfully by people who are firmly, even grossly, in contact with their own physicality.

As I have described in detail in *Another Mother Tongue* (in "Friction Among Women"), on occasion while making love with my lover, Paula Gunn Allen, I have experienced love as "a golden glow." Within the visual sensation we two call "psychic sex," we have been able to transmit images from one mind to the other and to enhance our own visions. This ability spills into our lives in general, enabling us, at times, to "talk" to each other over long distance.

Audre Lorde in her essay "Uses of the Erotic: The Erotic as Power" discusses at length the all-pervasive importance of recognizing and allowing the powers of the erotic to permeate every facet of our lives. She suggests the erotic as a golden color in an image of the yellow powder used briefly after World War II to give white margarine a butter color.[73]

If I myself have seen love on the psychic plane, seen/felt it as a brilliant yellow light which allowed me to speak to my lover though she was five hundred, or three thousand miles away — surely the great Sappho saw it also, saw it tenfold more clearly, born as she was into a culture that had named the very quality of Psyche herself. And H.D. saying she had seen Sappho, and that she wore a colorless seamless gown, predicted that the goddess would return as Psyche, the butterfly. H.D. also predicted that in the future artists would appear who could access the "overmind," or "love-mind," as she described it in *Notes on Thought and Vision.*

Suppose Sappho was describing having access to the godforce of Aphrodite on the psychic plane, through the medium of sexual and emotional love, visualized as a golden light, a golden nectar poured into a golden cup, a golden house, a golden throne on which the god sat, the vehicle by which she arrived into Sappho's mind. Suppose Sappho was decribing the sound that accompanied this vision from the astral plane, as a whirring like sparrow's wings.

In the most matter-of-fact imaginable way, as is appropriate in approaching those on the other side, in the higher mind, as it is sometimes called, Sappho asked Aphrodite for a favor:

> *Ornate-throned immortal Aphrodite, wile-weaving daughter of Zeus, I entreat you: do not overpower my heart, mistress, with ache and anguish, but come here, if ever in the past you heard my voice from afar and acquiesced and*

came, leaving your father's golden house, with chariot yoked: beautiful swift sparrows whirring fast-beating wings brought you above the dark earth down from heaven through the mid-air, and soon they arrived; and you, blessed one, with a smile on your immortal face asked what was the matter with me this time and why I was calling this time and what in my maddened heart I most wished to happen for myself: 'Whom am I to persuade this time to lead you back to her lover? Who wrongs you, Sappho? If she runs away, soon she shall pursue; if she does not accept gifts, why, she shall give them instead; and if she does not love, soon she shall love even against her will.' Come to me now again and deliver me from oppressive anxieties; fulfil all that my heart longs to fulfil, and you yourself be my fellowfighter.[74]

These are perfectly clear instructions to a god who approaches on the psychic plane, flowing down through the mid-air, from a golden house, manifesting with a smile, entreated directly and simply to do a certain favor. The words have the ring of the voices of teachers and spirit-guides heard in modern psychic readings: lovely, spare, descriptive, and to the point.[75]

In another fragment Sappho says that Love came down from heaven wearing a purple mantle. Suppose this is a description of a similar sort; that, caught deep in the emotion of love, she called on a god of the psychic dimension and was visited with a visualization of intense color, purple. Or perhaps she spotted a purple aura just outside Aphrodite's normal golden one. Or perhaps the aura was that of one of her lovers, was Love wearing a purple mantle.

Perhaps we are closer to recovering large portions of Sappho's world than we realize. By integrating our fragmented selves, and by inverting the patriarchal order and world view, we work to create a new paradigm, a new thought from Thought Woman's weaving basket, a new dream, a new web, a common language hitherto forgotten or suppressed, a common mind, a new possibility for recovering our highest apple: the special uses of love, beauty and intelligence with which it is possible to live lives of grace and meaning.

Notes & Bibliography

Notes Part I

1   Sappho, *Greek Lyric*, Vol. 1, David A. Campbell, trans., Harvard University Press, Cambridge, MA, 1982, p. 131.

    I appreciate the lovely interpretive translations of Sappho's work that have been done by Mary Barnard, Willis Barnstone, Susie Q. Groden and others I see occasionally. However I could not have done the particular comparisons in this book without a source that is simply a literal, word-for-word translation of Sappho's content. So I have used only one text for her words, D. A. Campbell's *Greek Lyric*, for which I am completely grateful.

2   Information thanks to Audre Lorde.

3   Sappho, 1982, op. cit., p. 57.

4   Ibid., p. 117.

5   Ibid., p. 67.

6   Suzy Q. Groden, *The Poems of Sappho*, Bobbs-Merrill, NY, 1966, p. xi, "During her lifetime Lesbos was in a state of political turmoil, and when the commoner Pittacus came to power, Sappho and others of the aristocratic party may have been forced to leave the island to live as exiles in Sicily." Ann Forfreedom, who I heard give a talk on the subject in San Diego in the early 1970's mentioned two exiles, and that Pittacus became a word meaning "tyrant."

7   David Robinson, *Our Debt to Greece and Rome*, Cooper Square, NY, 1963, p. 25.

8   Ibid., p. 24.

9   Elly Bulkin and Joan Larkin, eds. *Lesbian Poetry*, The Gay Presses of New York, NY, 1982.

10 Sappho, 1982, op. cit., p. 161.

11 I want to thank Robert Duncan for giving me this phrase.

12 Sappho, 1982, op. cit., p. 99.

13 John Boswell, *Christianity, Homosexuality and Social Tolerance*, Boswell, trans., University of Chicago Press, Chicago, 1980, p. 220.

14 Joanna Bankier and Diedre Lashgari, *Women Poets of the World*, Kenneth Rexroth and Ling Chung, trans., MacMillan, NY, 1983, pp. 24-25.

15 Paula Gunn Allen, *The Woman Who Owned The Shadows*, Spinsters Ink, San Francisco, 1983, pp. 155-156.

16 Sappho, 1982, op. cit., p. 173.

17 Contrast Dickinson's isolation and dependence on her family with Walt Whitman's uneasy freedom, on the road, rootless. The one was bound to a room in her father's house and the unrequited disappointed love she could not have and would not give up; the other poet was bound to a rootless, though magnificent road and lover after lover with whom he could not bond nor build permanent place.

   In their individual ways, they were both isolated, both lived in fragmented, incompleted worlds, both were outcasts from their society because of their chosen arts as well as their chosen loves, and both are currently emerging as the most important poets of the nineteenth century.

18 Adrienne Rich, *On Lies, Secrets and Silence*, W.W. Norton, NY, 1979, p. 176. For several years, Rich lived just up the road from Dickinson's Amherst, Massachusetts.

19 Lillian Faderman, *Surpassing the Love of Men*, William Morrow, NY 1981, p. 176.

20 Rebecca Patterson, *The Riddle of Emily Dickinson*, Cooper Square, NY, 1973. Patterson is of interest as the first person to point out the emotional attachments to women that are evident in Dickinson's work. But her painfully literal interpretations have become outdated by the more recent scholarship of Lillian Faderman, Paula Bennett and others. I found Patterson valuable for the details of Kate Scott's Lesbian life, and for several versions of the poetry itself that are more

entrancing to me than versions published in *The Complete Poems of Emily Dickinson*, Thomas H. Johnson, ed., Little Brown, Boston, 1951. According to Dickinson scholar Paula Bennett, although Scott and Dickinson had a tumultuous affair for two years, and Scott intermittently swirled like a disruptive whirlwind into Emily's life thereafter, Sue Gilbert Dickinson was the mainstay love of the poet's life. (Private conversation, thank you Paula Bennett.)

21 Patterson, ibid., p. 129.

22 Ibid., p. 125. Johnson (Dickinson, 1951, op. cit., p. 312.) used the version, "must be" to describe the North side of Emily's cottage.

23 Ibid., p. 226. Johnson has a different version ending "penury and home," op.cit., p. 572

24 Johnson, op.cit., p. 382. It is the center of three verses.

25 Ibid., p. 475.

26 Amy Lowell, *The Complete Poetical Works of Amy Lowell*, Houghton Mifflin, Boston, 1955, p. 212.

27 Ibid., p. 210.

28 Ibid., p. 213.

29 *The Penguin Book of Women Poets*, Carol Cosman, Joan Keefe and Kathleen Weaver, eds., Penguin Books, NY, 1978, p. 331. A similar thought was expressed at about the same time by Elsa Gidlow, writing in 1919 of both the threat of the streets, and of the Lesbian as a sinister, witchy robber:

> I have robbed the garrulous streets,
> Thieved a fair girl from their blight,
> I have stolen her for a sacrifice
> That I shall make to this night.
>
> I have brought her, laughing,
> To my quietly dreaming garden.
> For what shall be done there
> I ask no man pardon.

These two stanzas from "For the Goddess Too Well Known," is an early rendition of the theme of the Lesbian who rescues her lover from the oppression and "blight" of a masculine public world. This becomes a major theme for the work of literally dozens of Lesbian poets during the 1970's. The poem is in *Sapphic Songs*, (Druid Heights, Mill Valley, 1982), originally published in a collection in 1923.

30 Lowell, 1955, op. cit., "Frimaire," p. 219.

31 Ibid., p. 208.

32 Radclyffe Hall, *The Well Of Loneliness*, Avon Books, NY, 1975.

33 Gertrude Stein, *The Yale Gertrude Stein*, Richard Kostalanetz, ed., Yale University, New Haven, 1980, p. xix.

34 H.D., "Winter Love," *Hermetic Definition*, New Directions, NY, 1972, p. 97.

35 Judy Grahn, *The Work of a Common Woman*, Crossing Press, Trumansburg, 1984, p. 67.

36 Rita Mae Brown's *The Hand That Cradles The Rock* was published soon after (1972) on the East Coast. Elsa Gidlow, of course, had published overtly Lesbian poetry in the 1920's.

37 Paula Gunn Allen, "Beloved Women," *Lesbian Poetry*, op. cit., pp. 65-67 Also, "Beloved Women: Lesbians in American Indian Cultures," *Conditions 7*, Conditions, NY, 1981.

38 Interestingly, the poets who "came out" late in their careers, or who (in H.D.'s case) most severely covered the Lesbian content of their work, are all women with children, H.D., Rich, Lorde, Allen. The others: Dickinson (who did not cover up the Lesbianism of her words — others did it for her), Lowell, Stein, myself and Broumas, are all without children.

39 Audre Lorde, "Walking Our Boundaries," *The Black Unicorn*, W.W. Norton, NY, 1978, p. 39.

40 Grahn, 1984,op.cit., "A Woman Is Talking To Death," pp. 113-131. The subject of a bridge and the crossing over by Lesbians is treated caustically and personally in a complex poem by Los Angeles poet Eloise Klein Healy. Rigid movement politics ("Your fist and a finger always pointing.") are seen as the villain that closed the dialogue of an inter-cultural friendship; as with "A Woman Is Talking To Death,"

the bridge is the Bay Bridge, leading into San Francisco. The two women cannot reach the bridge, the poem says, because of an argument they are having on the on-ramp leading to it; they are separated by the argument, "a rope ladder suspended in cold green water." The poem ends wih desire for reconciliation: "We're bulldogs both of us. / Give in. I want to give in. / I miss imagining you. / Questions and answers. / I miss each of us pointing out / something." (from "What Is Left of Our History," unpublished ms.).

41 Olga Broumas, *Beginning With O*, Yale University, New Haven, 1977, p. 62.

42 Lorde, 1978, op.cit.,"Between Ourselves," pp. 112-114.

43 Audre Lorde, "October," *Chosen Poems, Old and New*, W.W. Norton, New York, 1982, p. 108. This poem was written in 1980.

44 Bankier and Lashgari, op. cit., pp. 24-25.

45 Lorde, 1978, op.cit., "Woman," p.82.

46 Broumas, 1977, op.cit., "Triple Muse," p. 9.

47 Rich, 1978, op.cit., p. 27.

48 Mary Carruthers refers to this as "eschatology."

49 Paula Gunn Allen, "Moonstream," *Skins and Bones*, Passion Press, San Francisco (forthcoming, 1985).

50 Adrienne Rich, "Twenty-One Love Poems," *Dream of a Common Language*, W.W. Norton, NY, 1978, pp. 35-36.

51 Ibid., "Trancendental Etude," p. 77.

52 Lorde, 1982, op.cit., p.114.

53 Grahn, 1984, op. cit. "She Who Poems," p. 95.

54 Ibid., p. 105.

55 Judy Grahn, *The Queen of Wands*, Crossing Press, Trumansburg, 1983, pp. 3-6.

56 Grahn, 1978, op.cit., 42.

57 Lorde, 1978, op. cit., "School Note," p. 55.

58 Paula Gunn Allen, "Red Roots of White Feiminism," in *Sinister Wisdom 25*, Winter, 1984, Sinister Wisdom, Rockland, Me., p. 34.

59 Grahn, 1984, op.cit., p. 69.

60 Broumas, 1977, op. cit., "Snow White," pp. 70-71.

61 Sappho, op.cit., p. 69.

Notes Part II

1 Sappho, *Greek Lyric*, David A. Campbell, trans., Harvard University Press, Cambridge, MA, 1982, p. 147.

2 Ibid., p. 155.

3 H.D., "The Wise Sappho," *Notes on Thought and Vision*, City Lights Books, San Francisco, 1982, pp. 58-59.

4 Sappho, 1982, op. cit., p. 67.

5 H.D., 1982, op. cit, p. 60.

6 Sappho, 1982, op. cit., p. 73.

7 Ibid., p. 121.

8 H.D., 1982, op. cit., pp. 65-66.

9 Jean Gould, *Amy: The World of Amy Lowell and the Imagist Movement*, Dodd, Mead and Co., NY, 1975, p. 319.

10 I learned the basics of my writing as a child, especially from Edgar Allan Poe, Alfred Lord Tennyson, Alfred Noyes and other balladeers, John Donne, ee cummings and Gertrude Stein.

11 Gould, op. cit., p. 180.

12 Amy Lowell, *The Complete Poetical Works of Amy Lowell*, Houghton Mifflin, Boston, 1925, p.443.

13 Gould, op.cit., pp. 180-181.

14 H.D., *Helen in Egypt*, New Directions, NY, 1961, p. 85.

15 Ibid., p. 103.

16 *The Penguin Book of Homosexual Verse*, Stephen Coote, ed., Penguin Books, Suffolk, England, 1983, pp. 272-273.

17 Gertrude Stein, "Lifting Belly," *The Yale Gertrude Stein*, Richard Kostelanetz, ed., Yale University Press, New Haven, 1980, pp. 45-47.

18 Gertrude Stein, "Poetry and Grammar," *Lectures in America*, Beacon Hill, Boston, 1935, p. 236.

19 Paula Gunn Allen tells me that she believes it was Timothy Leary who first coined the phrase "culture-trance." During the Sixties he taught that it could be broken through the carefully controlled use of mind-altering drugs, especially LSD.

20 The poster was taken from Sappho, "Translation #2," *Sappho, A New Translation*, Mary Barnard, trans., University of California Press, Berkeley, 1958.

21 Sappho, 1982, op. cit., p. 185.

22 Pat Parker, "GROUP," *Movement in Black*, Crossing Press, Trumansburg, 1983, p. 136-138.

23 Adrienne Rich, "Power and Danger: Works of a Common Woman," *The Work of a Common Woman*, The Crossing Press, Trumansburg, 1984, pp. 17-18.

24 Adrienne Rich, *The Dream of a Common Language*, W.W. Norton, NY, 1978.

25 Olga Broumas, "with the clear plastic speculum," *Lesbian Poetry*, Elly Bulkin and Joan Larkin, eds., The Gay Presses of N.Y., 1981, p. 211.

26 Olga Broumas, *Beginning With O*, Yale University Press, New Haven, 1977, p. 70.

27 Alice Bloch, "Six Years," *The Penguin Book of Homosexual Verse*, op. cit., p. 375.

28 Arlene Stiebel, "The Common Woman's Common Language: Poems of Rich and Grahn," unpublished ms., pp. 2-3.

29 Mary Carruthers, "The Re-Visioning of the Muse: Adrienne Rich, Audre Lorde, Judy Grahn, Olga Broumas," *The Hudson Review*, Vol. XXXVI, Number 2, Summer 1983, pp. 293-322.

30 Judy Grahn, "The woman whose head is on Fire," *The Work of a Common Woman*, op. cit., pp. 107-109.

31 Audre Lorde, "Meet," *The Black Unicorn*, W.W. Norton, NY, 1978, pp. 33-34.

32 Audre Lorde, *Chosen Poems, Old and New*, W.W. Norton, NY, 1982.

33 Paula Gunn Allen, *Shadow Country*, University of California, Los Angeles, 1982, pp. 132-136.

34 Judy Grahn, *The Queen of Wands*, Crossing Press, NY, 1982, pp. 22.

35 Sappho, 1982, op. cit., p. 133.

36 A "House of Women" who can call themselves "Africa" is described at length in Donna Allegra's poem "When People Ask," in *Lesbian Poetry*, op. cit., p. 257. "say you are Africa come calling. . . a house of sisters sat up telling each other. . . . "

37 Audre Lorde, "October," *Chosen Poems*, op.cit., pp. 108-109.

38 Paula Gunn Allen, "Some Like Indians Endure," *Skins and Bones*, Passion Press, San Francisco, (forthcoming, 1985).

39 Rich, 1978, op. cit., pp. 32-33.

40 Ibid., p. 36.

41 Paula Gunn Allen, "Grandmother," *Coyote's Daylight Trip*, La Confluencia, Albuquerque, 1978, p. 50.

42 Rich, 1978, op. cit., p. 34.

43 Lorde, 1978, op. cit., p. 88.

44 Ibid., "Dream/Songs from the Moon of Beulah Land I-V," p. 75.

45 Ibid., "The Women of Dan Dance With Swords In Their Hands To Mark The Time When They Were Warriors," p. 14.

46 Audre Lorde, *Zami, A New Spelling of My Name*, Crossing Press, Trumansburg, 1983.

Notes Part III

1 Sappho, *Greek Lyric, Vol. 1*, David A. Campbell, trans., Harvard University Press, Cambridge, MA, 1982, p. 131.

2 Ibid., p. 147.

3 Idem.

4 Ibid., p. 155.

5 Ibid., p. 69.

6 Ibid., p. 123.

7 Ibid., p. 101.

8 Ibid., p. 97.

9 Ibid., p. 161.

10 Ibid., p. 155.

11 Ibid., p. 109.

12 Ibid., p. 101.

13 Judy Grahn, "Sashay Down the Lavender Trail," *Another Mother Tongue*, Beacon Press, Boston, 1984, pp.1 − 19.

14 Sappho, 1982, op. cit., p. 133.

15 Ibid., p. 91.

16 Ibid., p. 119.

17 Ibid., p. 159.

18 Ibid., p. 99.

19 Emily Dickinson, *The Complete Poems of Emily Dickinson*, Thomas H. Johnson, ed., Little Brown, Boston, 1951, p. 109.

20 Ibid., p. 315.

21 Ibid., p. 219.

22 Ibid., p. 698.

23 Ibid., p. 153.

24 Ibid., p. 552.

25 Ibid., p. 378.

26 Ibid., p. 112.

27 Ibid., p. 259-260.

28 Amy Lowell, "Mise en Scene," *The Complete Poetical Works of Amy Lowell*, Houghton Mifflin, Boston, 1955, p. 210. Originally published in *Pictures of a Floating World*.

29 Idem.

30 H.D., "The Walls Do Not Fall," *Selected Poems of H.D.*, Grove Press, NY, 1957, p. 79.

31 Ibid., "Tribute to the Angels," pp. 89-93.

32 H.D., "Amaranth," *H.D.: Collected Poems 1912-1944*, New Directions, NY, 1983, pp. 310-315.

33 Idem.

34 H.D., *Notes on Thought and Vision*, City Light Books, San Francisco, 1982, pp. 21-22.

35 Ibid., pp. 22.

36 H.D., 1983, op. cit., "Halcyon," pp. 271-272.

37 Ibid., "Halcyon," p. 276.

38 Ibid., "Halcyon," p. 277.

39 Audre Lorde, *Chosen Poems — Old and New*, W.W. Norton, NY, 1982, p. 48.

40 Ibid., "The Winds of Orisha," pp. 48-49.

41 Joy Harjo, "Moonlight," *She Had Some Horses*, Thunder's Mouth Press, NY, 1983, p. 51:

> "I know when the sun is in China
> because the night shining other-light
> crawls into my bed. She is moon.
> Her eyes slit and yellow she is the last
> one out of a dingy bar in Albuquerque—
> Fourth Street, or from similar avenues
> in Hong Kong. Where someone else has also
> awakened, the night thrown back and asked,
> 'Where is the moon, my lover'?
> And from here I always answer in my dreaming,
> 'the last time I saw her was in the arms
> of another sky'."

42 Audre Lorde, *The Black Unicorn*, W.W. Norton, New York, 1978, p. 12.

43 Ibid., p. 6.

44 Ibid., pp. 48-50.

45 Ibid., pp. 14-15.

46 Olga Broumas, *Beginning With O*, Yale University, New Haven, 1977, pp. 7-8.

47 Mary Carruthers, "The Re-Visioning the Muse: Adrienne Rich, Audre Lorde, Judy Grahn, and Olga Broumas," *The Hudson Review*, Vol. XXXVI, Spring, 1983, pp. 308-309.

48 Broumas, 1977, op. cit., pp. 45-47.

49 Olga Broumas, *Pastoral Jazz*, Copper Canyon Press, Port Townsend, 1983, p. 21.

50 Ibid., p.45.

51 Ibid., p. 25.

52 Ibid., p. 56.

53 Adrienne Rich, *The Dream of a Common Language*, W.W. Norton, New York, 1978, p. 42.

54 Ibid., p. 45.

55 Ibid., p. 49.

56 Ibid., p. 30.

57 Adrienne Rich, *Sources*, Heyeck Press, Woodside, 1983, p. 31.

58 Judy Grahn, "She Who," *The Work of a Common Woman*, Crossing Press, Trumansburg, 1984, p. 157.

59 Ibid., p. 130.

60 Ibid., p.157.

61 Ibid., p. 146.

62 Ibid., pp. 135-158.

63 Judy Grahn, *The Queen of Wands*, Crossing Press, Trumansburg, 1982, pp. 88-89.

64 Judy Grahn, *The Queen of Swords*, forthcoming.

65 Paula Gunn Allen, private conversation.

66 Paula Gunn Allen, *Shadow Country*, University of California Press, Los Angeles, 1982, pp. 123-124.

67 Paula Gunn Allen, *Skins and Bones*, Passion Press, San Francisco, 1985.

68 Starhawk, "Consciousness, Politics and Magic," *The Politics of Women's Spirituality*, Charlene Spretnak, ed., Doubleday, NY, 1982, p. 177.

69 Allen, 1985, op. cit. (Originally published in "Feminary," Vol. 13, p. 6)

70 H.D.'s student, poet Robert Duncan, says she made the distinction very clear to him, that the "white island" is not Lesbianism itself. From a private conversation.

71 Carruthers, op. cit., p.305.

72 Sappho, 1982, op. cit., p. 57, "from the shimmering leaves the sleep of enchantment comes down." She is describing the apple orchard they keep especially for Aphrodite while inviting her to it.

73 Audre Lorde, "Uses of the Erotic: The Erotic as Power," *Sister Outsider*, Crossing Press, Trumansburg, 1984, pp. 53-59.

74 Sappho, 1982, op. cit., pp. 53-54.

75 John J. Winkler, classics scholar who has studied Sappho's work extensively, pointed out to me that the word translated as "fellow-fighter," and used by Sappho to describe the kind of relationship she desired from Aphrodite, is a Greek word of male bonding, male companions-in-arms, who were, generally speaking, also lovers. Private conversation.

Bibliography

Allen, Paula Gunn. *Skins and Bones*. San Francisco: Passion Press, 1985.

——. "Red Roots of White Feminism." *Sinister Wisdom* ©25. Rockland, Maine: Sinister Wisdom, Spring, 1984. pp. 34-46.

——. *The Woman Who Owned the Shadows*. San Francisco: Spinsters Ink, 1983.

——. *Shadow Country*. Los Angeles: University of California, American Indian Studies Center, 1982.

——. *Star Child*. Marvin, South Dakota: Blue Cloud Quarterly, 1982.

——. "Beloved Women: The Lesbian in American Indian Culture." *Conditions 7*, New York: Conditions, 1981. pp. 65-87.

——. "The Sacred Hoop: A Contemporary Indian Perspective on American Indian Literature," in *Literature of the American Indian: Views and Interpretations*, Abraham Chapman, editor. New York: New American Library, 1975. pp. 111-136.

Bankier, Joanna and Lashgari, Dierdre, eds. *Women Poets of the World*. New York: Macmillan Publishing Co., 1983.

Bogin, Meg. *The Woman Troubadours*. Scarborough, England: Paddington Press, Ltd., 1976.

Boswell, John. *Christianity, Social Tolerance, and Homosexuality*. Chicago: University of Chicago Press, 1980.

Broumas, Olga. *Pastoral Jazz*. Port Townsend, WA: Copper Canyon, 1983.

———. *Beginning With O*. New Haven: Yale University Press, 1977.

———. Unpublished prose ms.

Bulkin, Elly and Larkin, Joan, eds. *Lesbian Poetry*. New York: Gay Presses of New York, 1985.

Cameron, Anne. *Daughters of Copper Woman*. Vancouver, BC: Press Gang, 1981.

Carruthers, Mary J. "Adrienne Rich's 'Sources' ". *River Styx, No. 15*. St. Louis: Big River Association, 1984.

———. "The Re-Vision of the Muse: Adrienne Rich, Audre Lorde, Judy Grahn, Olga Broumas." *The Hudson Review*. New York: Summer 1983.

Coote, Stephen, ed. *The Penguin Book of Homosexual Verse*. Suffolk, England: Penguin, 1983.

Daly, Mary. *Gyn/Ecology: The Metaethics of Radical Feminism*. Boston: Beacon Press, 1978.

———. *Pure Lust*. Boston: Beacon Press, 1984.

Davis, Elizabeth Gould. *The First Sex*. New York: G.P. Putnam's Sons, 1971.

Dickinson, Emily. *The Complete Poems of Emily Dickinson*. Thomas H. Johnson, ed. Boston: Little, Brown & Co., 1951.

———. *Selected Poems and Letters of Emily Dickinson*. Robert N. Linscott, ed. New York: Doubleday, 1959.

Faderman, Lillian. *Surpassing the Love of Men*. New York: William Morrow and Company, 1981.

Gidlow, Elsa. *Sapphic Songs: Eighteen to Eighty*. Mill Valley, CA: Druid Heights Books, 1982.

Gould, Jean. *Amy: The World of Amy Lowell and The Imagist Movement*. New York: Dodd, Mead & Co., 1975.

Grahn, Judy. *The Work of a Common Woman*. Trumansburg, NY: Crossing Press, 1984. Originally published in 1978. A collection consisting of "The Common Woman Poems (1969), "She Who" (written in 1972), "A Woman is Talking To Death (1974) and "Confrontations With The Devil In The Form of Love," (written in 1977).

——. *Another Mother Tongue: Gay Words, Gay Worlds*. Boston: Beacon Press, 1984.

——. *The Queen of Wands*. Trumansburg, NY: Crossing Press, 1982.

Harjo, Joy. *She Had Some Horses*. New York: Thunder's Mouth, 1983.

Harrison, Jane Ellen. *Epilegomena to the Study of Greek Religion and Themis*. New York: University Books, 1962.

——. *Mythology*. New York: Harcourt, Brace and World, Inc., 1924.

H.D. *Collected Poems 1912-1944*. New York: New Directions, 1983.

——. *Bid Me To Live*. New York: Dial, 1983.

——. *Notes on Thought and Vision*. (Includes "The Wise Sappho," an essay.) San Francisco: City Lights Books, 1982.

——. *Trilogy*. New York: New Directions Press, 1973.

——. *Helen in Egypt*. New York: New Directions, 1961.

——. *Hermetic Definition*. New York: New Directions, 1958.

——. *Selected Poems of H.D.*. New York: Grove Press, 1957.

——. *Red Roses for Bronze*. Boston: Houghton Mifflin, 1931.

——. *Collected Poems of H.D.* New York: Liveright Publishing Co., 1925.

Lorde, Audre. *Sister Outsider*. Trumansburg, NY: Crossing Press, 1984.

——. *Chosen Poems — Old and New*. New York: W.W. Norton, 1982.

——. *Zami, A New Spelling of My Name*. Trumansburg, NY: Crossing Press, 1982.

——. *The Black Unicorn*. New York: W.W. Norton, 1978.

Lowell, Amy. *The Complete Poetical Works of Amy Lowell*. Boston: Houghton Mifflin, 1955.

——. *Pictures of the Floating World*. Boston: Houghton Mifflin, 1924.

Marks, Elaine. "Lesbian Intertextuality," in *Homosexualities and French Literature, Cultural Contexts/Critical Texts*. George Stambolian and Elaine Marks, eds. Ithaca, NY: Cornell University Press, 1979.

Ostriker, Alicia. *Writing Like A Woman*. Ann Arbor: University of Michigan Press, 1983.

Parker, Pat. *Movement In Black*. Trumansburg, NY: Crossing Press, 1983. (First published in 1978.)

Patterson, Rebecca. *The Riddle of Emily Dickinson*. New York: Houghton Mifflin Co., 1951.

Neumann, Erich. *The Great Mother*. Princeton: NJ: Princeton University Press, 1963.

Rich, Adrienne. *Sources*. Woodside, CA: Heyeck Press, 1983.

——. *A Wild Patience Has Taken Me This Far*. New York: W.W. Norton, 1983.

——. *On Lies, Secrets and Silence, Selected Prose 1966-1978*. Especially "Vesuvius at Home: The Power of Emily Dickinson," (1975) and "Power and Danger: Works of a Common Woman," (1977). New York: W.W. Norton, 1979.

——. *The Dream of a Common Language, Poems 1974-1977*. New York: W.W. Norton, 1978.

——. *Of Woman Born*. New York: W.W. Norton, 1977.

——. *Adrienne Rich's Poetry*. Barbara Harlesworth Gelpi and Albert Gelpi, eds. New York: W.W. Norton, 1975.

——. *Diving Into the Wreck*. New York: W.W. Norton, 1973.

Robinson, Janice S. *H.D., The Life and Work of an American Poet*. Boston: Houghton Mifflin, 1982.

Rothery, Guy Cadogan. *The Amazons in Antiquity and Modern Times.* London: Frances Griffiths, 1910.

Sappho. *Greek Lyric, vol. 1.* David A. Campbell, trans. Cambridge, MA: Harvard University Press, 1982.

——. *The Poems of Sappho.* Suzie Q. Groden, trans. New York: Bobbs-Merrill, 1966.

——. *Sappho.* Willis Barnstone, trans. Garden City, NY: Doubleday, 1965.

——. *Sappho: A New Translation.* Mary Barnard, trans. Berkeley: University of California Press, 1958.

Sewall, Richard B. *The Life of Emily Dickinson.* New York: Farrar, Straus and Giroux, 1980.

Sobol, Donald. *The Amazons of Greek Mythology.* South Brunswick: A.S. Barnes, 1972.

Spretnak, Charlene, ed. *The Politics of Women's Spirituality.* Garden City, NY: Doubleday, 1982.

Starhawk. "Consciousness, Politics and Magic." in *The Politics of Women's Spirituality*, Charlene Spretnak, ed. New York: Doubleday, 1982, p. 177.

Stein, Gertrude. *Fernhurst, Q.E.D. and Other Early Writings.* New York: Liveright, 1983.

——. *The Yale Gertrude Stein.* New Haven: Yale University Press, 1980.

——. *A Primer for the Gradual Understanding of Gertrude Stein.* Los Angeles: Black Sparrow Press, 1971.

——. *Lectures in America.* Boston: Beacon Hill, 1935.

Stiebel, Arlene. "The Common Woman's Common Language: Poems of Rich and Grahn." Unpublished paper.

Winkler, John J. Three lectures on Sappho delivered at New College of California, in San Francisco, Fall, 1983.

Photo: Irene Young

Judy Grahn has been active in the Gay movement for the past twenty years as a poet, publisher, and organizer. One of the foremost voices of Lesbian/feminism, her works include *The Common Woman Poems, Edward the Dyke,* and *The Queen of Wands,* and she is the editor of two books of short stories on women's lives. Her most recent book is the ground-breaking Gay cultural history, *Another Mother Tongue – Gay Words, Gay Worlds.* She teaches Gay and Lesbian studies in San Francisco.

Spinsters, Ink is a women's independent publishing company that survives despite financial and cultural obstacles. Our commitment is to publishing works of literature and non-fiction that are beyond the scope of mainstream commercial publishers. We emphasize work by feminists and lesbians.

Your support through buying our books or making donations will enable us to continue to bring out new books—to publish between the cracks of what can be imagined and what will be accepted.

For a complete list of our titles, please write to us.

Spinsters, Ink
803 De Haro Street
San Francisco, CA 94107